WRITING HORROR FICTION

Guy N. Smith

A & C Black · London

First published 1996
A & C Black (Publishers) Limited
35 Bedford Row, London WC1R 4JH

© 1996 Guy Smith Associates

ISBN 0–7136–4339–0

A CIP catalogue record for this book is available from the British Library.

Typeset in 10/12pt Palatino
Printed in Great Britain by Biddles Ltd, Guildford, Surrey

Contents

For Sandra Sharp, in appreciation of her tireless
efforts in running my fan club

Introduction

Why write horror? Simply because the subject fascinates you and therefore you will write better horror than you will any other genre.

People read horror for entertainment, they want to be frightened rather than to have to unravel some detective mystery before they reach the end of the book. That is not to say that your horror novel cannot be a mystery with a surprise ending, but the overall theme must be one of terror in its varying forms which we shall study during the course of this book. A horror fan pays money to be frightened, whether it is the cover price of a book, admittance to a cinema or the hire of a video. If that person is not scared by what he reads or views then he has not had value for money. It is the duty of the horror writer to ensure the reader receives value for money. That is the essence of the horror fiction writer's job and it applies to every writer in every field of fiction.

The borderline between horror, science fiction, fantasy and crime fiction is a very narrow one; often the categories overlap. However, Good is needed to counteract Evil, hence we have a story of conflict between the two and in the past the 'evil one' usually got his 'comeuppance'. That is, however, a stereotyped approach to horror writing and today that need not necessarily be the case; we have anti-heroes where evil triumphs. This makes horror all the more fascinating because the outcome of the story is not then predictable.

A horror writer must make every attempt to disturb his readership but this is not attained simply by writing pages and pages of graphic mutilation. There is an art in creating an atmosphere of spine-tingling horror without resorting to this crudity and one of the aims of this book is to teach the aspiring writer a craft which relies upon literary skills as opposed to basic accounts of blood and gore.

I know only too well from the many letters which I receive from my readers that there is a mistaken belief that I have some secret formula which has enabled me to produce successfully some 60-plus horror novels. This is not the case and I would like to state at the outset that no such proven secret exists. The whole essence of successful horror writing is in being able to come up with an original idea and expand and write it in such a way that it will appeal to those who buy the book.

I hope within these pages to convey the method by which success can be achieved. But that in itself is not sufficient. Somewhere along the long tortuous path that leads to publication, every writer needs a lucky break. I had that stroke of luck many years ago. May you, too, be as fortunate.

1

The development of horror fiction

When writing a horror novel the author has an obligation to disturb his readers. If, during the reading of your novel, their pulse rate does not quicken and they do not glance furtively around the room to satisfy themselves that there is nothing hidden in the shadows, then they most certainly will not buy your second book, and the possibility of future commissions will diminish rapidly.

The writer must always have his future in mind, his career will not be established, unless he is extremely lucky, on the strength of one book. Should that happen, though, then the first book needs to be a very good one. In other words, your novel must not be less than good and that is why so much time must be spent on researching and plotting. But we shall come to those aspects in due course; the most important thing of all at this early stage is that the aspiring writer has some knowledge of how horror fiction has developed over the last 150 years.

I choose to begin around 1840 because that was when Edgar Allan Poe began writing horror. Poe is arguably the doyen of horror writers; the fact that his works are still in print is proof enough that they have stood the test of time and competed favourably with many excellent writers who came after him.

1840-1900

The first horror story I ever read, at the age of twelve, made such an impression upon me that I have reread it many times and it never fails to bring a prickling sensation to the nape of my neck. In fact, as a result of my morbid fascination for it, I developed a phobia about the subject of the story, one that I have never really been able to overcome; the most awful fate that could befall me is that of being buried alive.

The story in question is *The Premature Burial*, published in 1844. The plot is incredibly simplistic; it is a straightforward account of a cataleptic who is mistaken for dead and buried alive. The prose is slow moving, there is none of today's terse writing with short, snappy sentences intended to convey escalating tension; it does not need them. Its secret is the awfulness of being trapped alive in a coffin below ground. Good descriptive prose creates atmosphere and tension, and conveys the sheer hopelessness of the victim. Had it been penned by a lesser writer than Poe then its credibility would have been lost. In fact, I doubt whether the modern reader would have had the opportunity to read it, it would long have been lost in the mists of obscurity of the last century.

Nevertheless, *The Premature Burial* has spawned many imitations over the years but they have faded into insignificance. Poe made the theme his own, many writers have imitated it. His writing conveys abject terror, there is no light relief in it. That was the hallmark of the nineteenth-century horror writer, he both depressed and terrified the reader.

Poe's opening sentence is a direct example of this: 'There are certain themes of which the interest is all-absorbing, but which are too entirely horrible for the purpose of legitimate fiction.' Later on in Chapter 5 we shall look at the importance of a first paragraph, one that is designed to grip the reader and promises the most awful things to come. Poe mastered this at the very onset of his writing, it is a valuable lesson to other writers.

Edgar Allan Poe had a distinct advantage over most other writers of the macabre - he was a manic-depressive, possibly because he suffered ill-health for most of his short life. This undoubtedly made him the writer he was. He died when he was 40.

He set not just a precedent in horror stories but a standard, one that others were not slow to capitalize upon. J. Sheridan Le Fanu was a contemporary of Poe's, born in 1814. Le Fanu's most famous work was *Uncle Silas* (1864). A descendant of Sheridan, Le Fanu had a literary upbringing. He began his career in journalism, founding the Irish *Evening Mail*, and it was upon his appointment as editor of the *Dublin University Magazine* that he seized the opportunity to publish his own supernatural stories. Like Poe, Le Fanu was a depressive. He developed the illness after the death of his wife in 1858 and this is when he wrote most of his macabre fiction. He based *Uncle Silas* on a story *Passage in the Secret History of an Irish Countess* which he had written earlier in his career. Le Fanu was the master of implied horror, the forerunner of our present trend in psychological horror.

The aforementioned writers, thus, had a common factor in that they were both depressives. Doubtless this state of mind helped them considerably to convey an atmosphere of gloom and terror in their stories. But they had several Victorian counterparts who also became legends in the horror genre and who did not spend their writing hours enshrouded in a cloud of deep depression.

No brief catalogue of authors who shaped the future of horror fiction would be complete without Mary Shelley. Her novel *Frankenstein, or a Modern Promotheus* is probably the most famous horror novel of all time but it is best known by the many film adaptations which often bear no relation to the book itself. Shelley's idea was spawned by a nightmare and was published in 1818. It was her only work of note; most certainly it helped to popularize horror fiction but innumerable stories about Frankenstein are probably more widely read than the book itself. In 1994 I wrote a Frankenstein story which was published in *The Mammoth Book of Frankenstein* (Robinson Publishing). The publication was successful, it features the original Shelley novel and then follows this up with a further 23 Frankenstein-related short stories. Yet again, the influence of the monster is evident, it is clearly immortal in the realms of horror fiction.

Charles Dickens was probably the most famous British novelist of the nineteenth century, renowned for a number of classical works so that his horror fiction is almost forgotten except by enthusiasts of the genre. His two best horror stories are undoubtedly *A Child's Dream of a Star* (1850) and *The Haunted House* (1859). Like most early horror writers, his theme was ghost stories which was also mirrored much more gently in probably his most famous novel of all, *A Christmas Carol* (1843). The Victorians had an insatiable appetite for spooky yarns and most writers were influenced by this, realising the effect on sales. As a result there was a wealth of supernatural fiction during this era, the beginning of a trend which still exists today.

A ghostly story will help increase the saleability of a book but after a century and a half of variations of a theme, the beginner is advised to try to find a new slant on the headless spook which walks the ramparts of the ruined castle at midnight!

Charles Dickens, as well as writing, edited two magazines, namely *Household Words* and *All the Year Round*, which ran for two decades. One of his contributors was Wilkie Collins, who doubtless learned his craft from 'the Master' and himself produced some weird short stories. Dickens used these magazines to publish his own weird fiction.

It was another fifty years, however, before another novel was to be published which would remain in print until the present day. This was the infamous *Dracula* by Bram Stoker, published in 1897.

It was destined to become the most famous of all vampire stories. Stoker was unable to repeat his feat, the nearest he came to it was with *The Lair of the White Worm* (1911).

More and more writers were producing horror fiction; authors who were better known for works of adventure, detective fiction and romance added their names to the growing roll of writers of weird fiction.

Guy de Maupassant was a writer in much the same mould as Poe and Le Fanu in so much as he feared madness and this was mirrored in his fiction. This is clearly reflected in *The Horla* and *Who Knows?*, which is written in the first person by a man in a mental institution. Maupassant, like Poe, died young, his terror of insanity had driven him mad. He was a literary writer and but for his early death would doubtless have risen to even greater heights.

H. Rider Haggard, renowned for those classic adventure stories of Africa, *King Solomon's Mines* and *She*, chose to write his own brand of horror into that same African setting with *The Witch's Head* (1885).

Guy Boothby, who is primarily known for his detective novels, also trod the dark paths of weird fiction with *A Bid for Fortune* (1895). His Dr Nikola was an occult adventurer and featured in a series of books. Many of Boothby's novels straddle the border between detective fiction and weird fiction. He was yet another promising writer who died at an early age.

Robert Louis Stevenson achieved fame with *Treasure Island* (1883) and was, surprisingly, writing horror within three years of its publication. *The Strange Case of Dr Jekyll and Mr Hyde* (1888) is one of the horror classics of all times and has been adapted and abridged in many forms. Like Poe and Guy de Maupassant before him, Stevenson was influenced by the dark corners of his own mind. Jekyll and Hyde was spawned by his own nightmares but he was to follow this up with some short horror stories. He suffered from tuberculosis and died when he was only 44.

Sir Arthur Conan Doyle is best known for his creation of the character, Sherlock Holmes, who is without doubt the most famous fictional detective of all time. And yet many of these stories are undoubtedly horror with a criminal thread interwoven. What could be more horrible than the deadly swamp adder in *The Speckled Band* slithering from the adjoining room to bite its unsuspecting victim in the dead of night? Or the spectral *Hound of the Baskervilles* baying on the lonely moorland after dark? There are many other horror elements interwoven with the Holmes' stories but, either deliberately or subconsciously, Doyle infiltrated the realms of weird fiction.

There is *The Parasite* (1894), but my own favourite is *The Horror of the Heights*, about a pilot, when aviation was in its infancy, who flew to a height of 7 miles in order to discover what unimaginable horror was preying on pilots above the clouds. He even took a double-barrelled shotgun along with him in his aircraft in order to deal with whatever he might discover up in 'the heights'!

1900-1960

The early part of the twentieth century spawned a wealth of horror fiction, much of it by authors who are household names today. Algernon Blackwood began writing for British magazines following his return from the USA just before the turn of the century. Blackwood uses the theme of an occult investigator in his book *John Silence* (1908) which was based on Blackwood's own paranormal experiences. Much of his magazine fiction was later published in bound collections. His few novels are virtually forgotten but his short fiction is constantly reprinted.

Although generally regarded as one of the best writers in the horror field, Arthur Machen's fame rests almost solely on his novel *The Bowmen* (1914). His work is widely read and extensively collected today, probably because of his commitment to the supernatural theme. He wrote with authority and clearly believed in the supernatural. In *The Inmost Light* (1894), Machen warns readers not to become involved in the occult which, surely, is a sign that he believed in it.

Walter de la Mare is most famous as a poet and children's author but he also wrote some excellent macabre fiction. I have reread *The Return* many times, a novel about a man who visits a churchyard and becomes possessed by the spirit of a suicide. Walter de la Mare was a prize-winning author and it is his prose which is most compelling. Here is a classic example of a literary writer creating a memorable novel out of a very ordinary idea, one that has been used countless times but rarely with such compulsion.

William Hope Hodgson is surely the master of nautical horror stories. As a youth he ran away to sea and his experiences were invaluable to him as a writer. Again we have an occult investigator character in *Carnacki, the Ghost-Finder* (1913), but Hodgson's most famous novel is undoubtedly *The House on the Borderland* (1908). Above all else, Hodgson's work is an example of how first hand research is the making of a book. A good plot can appear very shallow without authentic detail and background.

1913 saw the emergence of 'Doctor Fu Manchu', created by Sax

Rohmer. Purists will argue as to whether the series of books featuring Dr Fu Manchu are horror or mystery fiction. I will hedge my bets, they incorporate both genres just as Doyle did on occasions with Sherlock Holmes. Rohmer was a journalist but found fame and fortune with Dr Fu Manchu, the Oriental master criminal who is relentlessly hounded by Mr Nayland Smith of Burma.

Rohmer's research was meticulous. He based Dr Fu Manchu upon a Chinese master criminal who operated in London's Chinatown. However, in order to bring his character to life, he paid a petty criminal in the docklands to obtain for him a view of this man. It was achieved after a long wait on a foggy night; just one glimpse, that was all that Rohmer needed.

Howard Phillips Lovecraft (1890-1937) was another writer very much in the Edgar Allan Poe tradition and was clearly influenced by Poe. Lovecraft suffered from ill health and was yet another genius who was also a depressive. He wrote frequently of grim dark places from which there was no escape. Innsmouth, a coastal township, was one such place, its inhabitants having an affinity with creatures of ancient evil that inhabited the ocean and crawled ashore after dark. In *Dagon* (1923), Lovecraft wrote in typical depressing vein:

> I am writing this under an appreciable mental strain since by tonight I shall be no more. Penniless, and at the end of my supply of the drug which alone makes life endurable, I can bear the torture no longer; and shall cast myself from this garret window into the squalid street below.

It is worth noting that in that opening paragraph Lovecraft sets the scene, conveys the state of mind of his character (and probably of his own), as well as his surroundings, the mental torture in a garret in a squalid street, and the contemplation of suicide. The horror and utter degradation of it all has been successfully conveyed in those few sentences.

Yet Lovecraft had an author's licence which would not be valid today. On more than one occasion he writes of 'a horror too awful to describe'. Today's readership is both critical and discerning, if something was that awful then they would demand that it was described fully. References to unknown horrors would not go unchallenged.

The Cthulhu Mythos stories are undoubtedly Lovecraft's best known work and are now very successfully continued by Brian Lumley, Basil Copper and Fred Chappell. Recently, I was given the opportunity to write in this style when I was asked to contribute a story to *Shadows Over Innsmouth,* (Innsmouth was the scene of Lovecraft's story *The Shadow Over Innsmouth*). *Shadows Over Innsmouth* is a volume of short stories, all written by contemporary horror writers, and written in the Lovecraft style. All stories had to be set in Innsmouth. Mine was *Return to Innsmouth* ('what happened afterwards'). It was an intriguing exercise and I enjoyed the change of style. This anthology was published by Fedogan & Bremner, Minneapolis.

The pulp magazines

Before we look at the post war development of horror fiction, we must examine the influence that the 'pulps' (magazines produced from recycled paper but with magnificent covers) had on horror. Pulps were published from the 1920s until their demise in the 1950s. Without this proliferation of popular fiction it is doubtful whether many of the writers whom we read today would have become established. Talented writers seized upon an unprecedented opportunity; editors were prepared to buy their work, as many stories as they could write in a lot of cases, and often for as little as one or two cents a word. In order to make a living from writing an author had to write prolifically, quantity came a close second to quality. Titles came and went, there were British reprints of American titles, and during World War II, pulps were used as ballast in some of the cargo ships returning across the Atlantic. It was the golden age of mass market publishing and horror fiction was undergoing a revitalization. But, with paper shortages a thing of the past, those days of cheap but attractive magazines went into decline in the 1950s.

In many ways Lovecraft shaped horror fiction for the years which followed, spawning fearsome monsters which multiplied and mutated in many forms with the help of countless later writers. But without *Weird Tales*, the legendary horror pulp magazine which still exists today, albeit in a different style and format, H.P. Lovecraft's work might never have achieved a wide readership. Writers such as Manly Wade Wellman, Theodore Sturgeon, August Derleth and Robert Bloch graced its recycled pages in the early days before they became household names.

Their success, and that of *Weird Tales*, was due to the fact that they were accomplished writers who were given the opportunity to develop their talents when a ready market existed for bizarre fiction. It seemed that the appetite of the readership was insatiable.

The *Not at Night* series, edited by Christine Campbell Thomson, was published between the two world wars and carried many reprints of stories from *Weird Tales*. They make worthwhile reading for collectors unable to find, or afford, original copies of *Weird Tales*. Indeed, the 'Not at Night' books are a highly collectable series themselves.

The pulp-era was coming to an end by the early 1950s and was rapidly being replaced by 'digest' magazines (paperback-size anthologies). Often these continued with the same titles and authors as their predecessors but they did not have the same appeal. The market for short stories was already showing signs of going into decline.

Sadly, for today's writers, the short story market is a contracting one. The war, with its paper shortages, brought an abrupt halt to this mushroom publishing of magazines and many of the pulps did not resurface after the end of the war, whilst those that survived discovered that the readership was a more discerning one. Whilst the works of Poe, Lovecraft and a few of their contemporaries remain immortal classics, the trend was towards more believable horror. Monsters were required to have reasonably credible reasons for their existence, scientific facts had to be substantiated, albeit fictitiously. Readers had enquiring minds, they would no longer accept 'horrors too awful to describe'.

The 1950s saw a new trend in paperback publishing, publishers sprang up virtually overnight. Some lasted a few years, others disappeared after half a dozen titles. The imprint which published over a hundred horror titles was Badger (John Spencer & Co). Most of their novels were written by one man, Lionel Fanthorpe, under about twenty pseudonyms as well as his own name. These books had a variety of occult themes, were crammed with action and the characters were believable. They were exceptionally good novels and I read them avidly. Many years later I met Fanthorpe and a friendship developed which still exists today. As well as the Badger Supernatural Series, Fanthorpe also wrote many of the Badger Science Fiction Series. At one point he was producing a 40,000-word novel every week!

But mushrooming publishing had had its day by the mid 1960s; those publishers which survived after saturation point settled down to producing fewer books, concentrated on market research in order to compete with the growing threat of television. Visual horror was replacing the written story.

The early 1950s saw the birth of one of the last pulp-style magazines - the *London Mystery Magazine*. Here, indeed, was a market for aspiring writers, a mixture of horror and crime fiction. As with the pulps, many of its contributors went on to become successful novelists.

Most of the stories had 'twist' endings, something that was becoming ever more fashionable so that this ploy became the criterion for acceptance. It was the task of the writer to deceive the reader right up to the very end. My own writing career was beginning to take off in the 1970s and *London Mystery Magazine* was virtually the only market place available for the short story fiction I was producing in between novels. I sold 18 stories to the magazine between 1972 and when it folded in 1982.

1960-1996

Alongside these last surviving short story magazines was the prestigious *Pan Book of Horror Stories*. This was first launched in 1959 under the editorship of Herbert van Thal. The standard was high and the series achieved a worthwhile status in the league of short horror fiction. It lasted thirty years, the title was changed to *Dark Voices* in 1990 under the editing team of Stephen Jones and David Sutton, and then dropped by Pan in 1994. It is a sad reflection on the current popularity of short horror fiction. However, Gollancz took over the prestigious title and published it as *Dark Terrors* for Halloween 1995 so there is still a small market available for the writer of this type of fiction but it is a much harder one to crack. Only the best horror writing will survive in this field.

Spanning the changing face of horror fiction was the writer, Dennis Wheatley, who also wrote adventure, spy and historical fiction. In 1935 *The Devil Rides Out* was published, a novel that was destined to create an interest in the occult. Wheatley followed this with more black magic themes, his last work of fiction in the genre being *The White Witch of the South Seas* in 1968. His fiction established him as a leading authority on the occult and in 1971 he published a comprehensive reference work on the subject entitled *The Devil and All His Works*. His books inspired innumerable occult novels by other authors over the sixty years following publication of *The Devil Rides Out*.

In the early 1970s a separate genre was born within the horror field, short books (around 40,000 words), with basic plots but very explicit in sex and gore. They were dubbed 'Nasties'. It was a boom industry within the industry, virtually every original paperback publisher fought for a stake in the lucrative market. In effect, it was the pulp era reborn in paperback format with those appealing lurid covers which were often as important to sales as the stories themselves. This heralded a new batch of horror writers, some who were to outlast the trend and go on to higher things.

James Herbert's *The Rats* led to several sequels and then acted as a springboard to establish him as a leading horror novelist. Shaun Hutson's *Slugs* opened up new realms of revulsion, whilst Ramsey Campbell went quietly along with quality books. My own *Night of the Crabs* became an overnight bestseller in 1976 and led to five sequels and around 60 other horror novels.

Saturation point was inevitable. In the early 1980s I was invited to a publisher's Halloween party to launch yet another list of 'nasties'. Almost everybody there was either already writing nasties or had been commissioned to write one; for some it was their first book, bought on a brief synopsis. Unfortunately, for the novice writer, this kind of thing just does not happen today.

But within a couple of years or so the bubble had burst. Again the readership was looking to break new boundaries, they demanded quality rather than quantity. The remainder baskets were full to overflowing.

It was time to change yet again.

The American influence

Just as Edgar Allan Poe and Howard Phillips Lovecraft shaped the future of horror fiction in its formative years, again it was an American writer who brought about yet another change of direction. Stephen King changed the face of horror when *Carrie* was published in 1974. His books were refreshingly different from all that had gone before. Psychological horror began to make a real impact. No longer were victims chased and mutilated by bizarre monsters dreamed up by a writer who did not have to explain or justify his creations; instead they were pursued by the figments of the mind, often their own. It was insidious, thought-provoking and much more frightening.

King's next books, *Salem's Lot* (1975) and *The Shining* (1977) set the pattern for longer books. The 40,000-word novels were gone, their successors stretched to 100,000-words plus, and they were growing in size all the time. King's *The Stand* ran to a staggering 700 pages and some of his later books were to exceed 1,000.

Stephen King was one of the first writers to use brand names extensively and this was yet another factor in his incredible success. It added authenticity to a well-written story, that touch of realism which enabled readers to identify even more with his books. His characters were ordinary people, the victims could just as easily have been the readers he targeted. It was a well-researched policy which made him the world's bestselling author, both in the horror field and all other genres.

His colloquial style was accepted now, whereas previously it would have been criticized heavily. He launched horror fiction towards new horizons, exploded many of the taboos that had restricted it in the past, such as graphic descriptions of carnage. His novel *Gerald's Game* (1992) has a bondage theme which would have caused an outcry two or three decades ago.

Other horror writers who are making their mark include Dean Koontz, who wrote innumerable books under various pseudonyms before receiving recognition, and William W. Johnstone who is one of America's most prolific authors. Johnstone has written westerns, adventure, truckers and romantic fiction as well as horror. His output is phenomenal.

Horror writers needed to change to survive. The 'western' genre had collapsed and died and horror was in danger of doing just that. Only a fool would attempt to imitate King but writers needed to come up with new ideas and present them in a different way. Apart from the excellent Lovecraftian-style 'Necroscope' books written by Brian Lumley, today's horror novels are almost exclusively set in modern times. Why?

1. Because readers like to identify with the world they know and its everyday characters.

2. Because real life horror is far more terrifying than anything the pulps ever produced.

The aspiring writer is urged to read both historical and modern horror novels. He or she needs to have an insight into the prose and styles of Poe and Lovecraft, to see how wordage was churned out in the boom years, and then to appreciate how discerning readers have become in recent times. Writing has progressed in much the same way as stage and screen; characters are portrayed as we see them around us, melodrama is no longer acceptable. Dialogue should be written as we hear it spoken, it is far more effective that way.

Sub-plots are all part and parcel of modern literature, Poe and his contemporaries neither needed nor used them, but in modern horror fiction an extra-marital affair running parallel with some world threatening saga can be made to increase the atmosphere of tension as well as evoking that human touch to the story which is so necessary to create realism. Often sub-plots are a major factor in producing a novel of mega-selling potential.

It is important to familiarize oneself with today's bestselling horror novels before attempting to write one, and also to have some insight into how the genre has changed and developed since the 1840s. Stories which frightened their readers a century or more ago would still do so today; they would just have to be presented differently.

It is said that there are only seven original storylines; every story ever written is but a variation of one of those seven.

2

Expanding an idea

Where do you get your ideas from?'

Virtually every interviewer, whether radio, television or newspaper, has asked me that question. Fans write in and ask me, friends ask me. Everybody asks me.

Until fairly recently it was one of those questions that I answered vaguely, because I didn't know. I had never really stopped to think about it. If the ideas dried up, I would be out of work. I just had to keep coming up with them.

Dreaming up ideas

To some extent ideas are a systematic process with me. Something occurs to me and I jot it down for future reference. I have never woken up in the middle of the night and scrawled something on the wall behind the bed in case I may have forgotten it in the morning. In Chapter 1 we saw how Mary Shelley and Robert Louis Stevenson wrote two of the all-time horror classics inspired by nightmares. Well, a similar thing happened to me a few years ago . . .

I had a recurring nightmare over a period of several weeks. Somebody or something with rasping breath shuffled its way down the corridor towards the bedroom; the door was edged open a little way but whoever it was didn't enter. My usual reaction to a nightmare is to become aggressive; according to my wife I shout incoherent threats and toss about in the bed. As I did so in these instances and, as on many occasions before, she thumped me awake.

The nightmare intrigued me. Who or what was it outside the bedroom door? There was only one way to find out so I requested Jean to tolerate my abuse for once and perhaps that way the dream would be brought to a conclusion by the nocturnal entity coming inside the bedroom where I could see it. She agreed, thinking the whole business was extremely funny.

It was some weeks before I had the dream again. Now the strange thing is that this time in my dream I was feigning sleep in an attempt to fool the intruder. The door creaked open, the shuffling footsteps entered. And that was when I leaped up in bed and viewed this ghastly near-skeletal figure, clad in a shabby raincoat and a greasy trilby hat which was pulled down in a futile attempt to hide its cadaverous features from me. It was clearly terrified of me, cowered back against the fitted wardrobe. I shrieked in incoherent anger and was actually in the process of getting out of bed, my intention being to get my hands round that scrawny neck, when Jean grabbed me, yelled at me to wake up. A great pity, but, no matter, I had seen all that I needed to see.

As a result, the idea for my book *The Cadaver* was born. It was a most profitable nightmare. And it never returned, not even during the writing of the book when my concentration was focused on it for hours at a time.

Ideas from characters

Sometimes a character is born before a book. I remember going to a wedding once when a man walked into church wearing a black jacket, jeans and a matching black fedora. He sat in a pew just behind me and, out of the corner of my eye, for he had already aroused my interest, I was somewhat surprised to see a cigarette dangling from his lips. In fact, the vicar came down the aisle and requested him not to smoke in church. It was some months afterwards, when the bride and groom brought this fellow to visit us, that he confessed that the cigarette was only a chocolate one!

The guy just had to be a book, I didn't know whether to use him as the good guy or the bad guy, I didn't even have a plot but I did have something definite to work on. So, *The Black Fedora* was written and then its sequel *The Knighton Vampires*. Initially, I saw him as a sinister character but then I decided that he had to be a hero. I hedged my bets: in the first book the reader is fooled (I hope!) into thinking that he's the baddie but he turns out to be an undercover cop. I think he'll go into a few more books. I'm really glad that I went to that wedding.

Rarely do ideas jump up and hit me out of the blue. I can never recall having had an idea during gardening or any similar chore. Simply because I'm too engrossed in what I'm doing. But some of my best ideas have come to me when I've been driving on a long journey on my own. I don't get them on trains or buses because I'm usually writing, roughing out some text to put on screen when I get home. I find a long car journey relaxing and inspiring, when it's away from the bulk of the traffic. Everybody thinks about something during driving; I let my thoughts wander, I don't channel them unless they throw up something specific. I let them roll and, when I'm least expecting it, something pops up and hits me. Many of the ideas for my early horror books were spawned in the car.

Ideas never occur when one needs them. If I were stuck for one, I guarantee that it would elude me mischievously. That is why any worthwhile idea is worth noting when it occurs for it will surely be useful at a later stage.

Stuck for ideas

It is very frustrating when an idea just won't come. The harder you try, the more it eludes you.

Reading can be a good source for ideas but one must be careful not to be influenced by another author's work. Remember, that plot is dead, the author has already used it and 'rip-offs' won't do you any favours. Sometimes, though, a situation within a book leads to an idea for another novel totally unrelated to the one you are reading.

I am always wary of my subconscious. When an idea springs to mind my first thought is whether I have read it somewhere, perhaps the blurb on the back of a book which I have picked up and browsed through in a bookshop and then put back. I have a retentive memory but I don't always trust it! In this case, I make a few notes in the notebook which I always carry with me and then leave it for some time. If the idea still grabs me in six months' time then I'll work further on it. Usually, then, I will remember if it has come from a dubious source.

Let's consider a negative situation: you are really stuck for an idea (and I'm never in favour of contrived ideas) and you are frustrated because you are unable to come up with something. All you need is a blank sheet of paper and a pencil. Shut yourself in a room well away from telephones, television and all other modern distractions. Head the sheet up 'Horror Ideas'. At least that way you have made a start!

Next: what kind of horror would you like to write? Psychological, occult, rampaging mutated monsters? Choose one of these and write it beneath your heading. Who knows, a provisional title might spring to mind with it. If it does, you are really on to a bonus. At least you know now what you want to write.

Still stuck? Okay, go for a character as I mentioned on page 16, somebody you have met or know, and work on it. That just might spawn a plot.

Phobias

Guy de Maupassant used his own phobia, his fear of madness, to its full potential. Do you have a phobia? If so, jot it down, write something about it. Suppose your worst fear came true. You shudder, but you are well on the way to producing a worthwhile idea.

One of my own phobias arose from the small underground reservoir that is our water supply. Every so often, more frequently in dry weather, it is necessary to inspect the water level and the only way to do this is to open the heavy concrete hatch and take a look down inside. It is deep and dark down there, there isn't even a ladder going down into the depths. If I chanced to fall in, I'd never get out, nobody would hear my cries for help. The thought used to send me cold, I just hated checking that reservoir.

Until the day that I used it in a book! The phobia is quite illogical, really, I would have to jump in deliberately; that never occurred to me until I wrote about it. It produced a good scenario in a book and I was never troubled by my fear again.

So, as a yardstick, write about whatever it is that you are most frightened of. In my own experience, one idea leads to another.

Scrapbooks

I shall mention these again in Chapter 4 covering the importance of research, but my library of scrapbooks (a small shelved alcove in one of the bedrooms) is invaluable for a twofold purpose.

Each scrapbook is clearly headed and numbered in sequence under a specific title. For example:

Natural Horrors: (includes plagues, earthquakes)

Serial Killers: (the borderline between atrocious crimes and horror is very narrow). This one contains every press cutting of the Fred/Rosemary West saga from the time the first body was unearthed until the conclusion of the trial. There will be more than enough books written on the Wests but a horror writer needs to know the depths of depravity which his characters might plumb. As they say, truth is stranger than fiction.

Animal Horrors: those straightforward novels of 'creatures on the rampage' may well come back into vogue. I collect accounts of big cats, giant squids, a plague of bullfrogs in the UK etc.

Police procedure: a writer needs to know how the police operate, and regulations are changing all the time. DNA has changed the face of all novels which involve police work, for example. Police methods will feature in many horror novels, you have to keep up to date. You must get it right or the credibility of everything else you write in the book will be destroyed.

The Loch Ness Monster: I am intrigued by this unsolved mystery and maybe I'll write something around it one day. Far better to accumulate the research as it becomes available.

General Research: something you may or may not need. This includes articles that interest you when you read them in your newspaper. Throw them away and you will forget them. They are worth pasting in.

UFO Sightings: this may well be more for the science fiction writer but, again, it could just feature in a future horror book. I restrict my scrapbooking to 'sightings'.

There are other scrapbooks which have helped in the past and may do so again; executions and war criminals record man's inhumanity to man. As in the case of the Wests and others, you'll have to write about it sometime if you are going to write horror. Collect articles now and they are there for when you need them.

My wife and I have a newspaper each every day. I am well aware of the various aspects of horror which relate to my books, ie the occult, natural horrors (ecological disasters, escaped wild animals etc.), psychological, plus a few sections that provide sub-plots if not a full book. My scrapbooks are headed and filed, it is important when you cut and paste every day to be able to find whatever you have saved.

Research is one reason for my painstaking mutilation of the dailies: ideas may also spring from them. So if you are not already a 'scrapbooker', start now. Clip and paste anything relating to horror. Make a neat job of it; it is, in fact, a book you are compiling and if it is easy to read then you will be more inclined to do so.

In any case, my scrapbooks make fascinating reading. It is intriguing to look back upon some event which you have virtually forgotten. Perhaps some conclusion has arisen from what was then a mystery; you have the nucleus of a fictional adaptation of macabre happenings.

But, be very careful, use your pastings only as a guide, what is in the paper is fact and concerns real people. You don't want a libel suit! Furthermore, the facts will already be known to the public at large, you have to present your readers with fiction. For example, I collected a piece about a tanker of toxic weedkiller which was involved in an accident and the weedkiller spilled and contaminated a nearby lake. I adapted that idea so that the lake became a reservoir which supplied a city with its drinking water. My weedkiller didn't dissolve and become harmless in such a volume of water - it formed a slick, went down the pipes and came out of household taps! The book, *Thirst*, sold 100,000-plus copies and I wrote a sequel. And all because I cut out a half column from a newspaper.

Travel

The more you travel, the more likely you are to come up with ideas for your proposed book. I don't mean exploring distant lands, although that is an excellent thing if you can afford it, just excursions beyond your normal routine journeys to work.

You will need somewhere to set your book and that is best done in surroundings you know. So this may be a jump ahead of the procedure but there is always the chance that a location might spark off an idea. Some building, perhaps an incident you witness in the street. Who knows? The more you travel, the more you see of life, and fiction is but an extension of reality. Truth can be a good starting place for your proposed novel.

As well as a notebook, I always carry a small loaded pocket camera. Mostly I use it for research but it is handy to snap something you may witness. It is always far easier to compile your idea from a photograph than from memory. Perhaps a location gives a hint of an idea but you are not sure exactly what. A detailed photograph will always aid a fertile imagination.

Imagination

Your imagination is a valuable asset, don't be afraid to let it run riot. I still have one of my school reports dating back to when I was about ten years of age. In the 'comments' column, my English teacher had written 'writes good English but lacks imagination'! I did not actually lack imagination but I was too inhibited to put it down on paper. I guess I saved it all up until I left school.

It was my mother who encouraged me and nurtured my boyhood imagination. She was a pre-war historical novelist and undoubtedly understood when others scoffed. Between the ages of ten and fourteen I was fascinated by the weekly comics and boys' story papers which were on sale. There was a wealth of well-written stories in the latter, as opposed to comic strips in the former, tales of piracy, adventure, westerns, detective and even horror! I well recall the story of a giant mole that existed deep in a maze of tunnels in a coal mine. Such was my fascination that I did gardening chores for neighbours to earn enough money to buy around a dozen papers a week, as well as paying for my twice-weekly cinema visits. My father and my headmaster poured scorn upon the 'rubbish' I was reading, I was forbidden to take any of these publications to school.

My mother thought otherwise but didn't dare say so. She suggested that I produce a weekly comic of my own and she would buy it off me for sixpence (old money, of course!). I did just that, I wrote and illustrated a comic every week (it ran to 52 issues without a break). She gave them all back to me years later.

Those boyhood ideas were all spawned from the comics and story papers I read, not plagiarised, I hasten to add, but the heroes of those days were stereotyped and I did not have much difficulty in creating my own similar characterization. The plots were all my own but, there again, cowboys, pirates, highwaymen and the like all had very similar adventures.

I cannot stress too strongly the benefits from just sitting down and writing. Make your first effort a 'trial run'. I wrote a few horror stories in my comics, I was learning with every one I wrote. My amateur apprenticeship served me well. I allowed my imagination to run riot in the full knowledge that nobody apart from my mother would read what I had written. It is well worth a try before you make your first serious attempt to submit your work to a publisher. Furthermore, those initial ideas may well develop later.

Just an idea

When a film company buys the film rights of a book, it is the idea which they are buying; the movie often bears little resemblance to the original novel. That puts the value of an idea into perspective. Ideas are the essence of any book you propose to write but it is how they are used that matters. Thousands of superb ideas have been wasted by authors over the years simply because they have not thought them through thoroughly. Consequently, those manuscripts have never progressed further than the editorial desk.

Find an idea, jot it down and then think about it, exploring every variation. If you go for the first plot that springs to mind you will probably end up with a wad of rejection slips. That original idea might only be the nucleus of something that will launch you into full-time writing.

Don't rush to start your book. A few weeks, even months, will not make any difference. Far rather success later than failure now.

3

Characterization

During the 1950s new paperback publishers were springing up almost weekly, as we mentioned in Chapter 1, but there were very few memorable characters in the books. It seemed that the storyline was all important and it was sufficient just to have silhouettes flitting through the pages with few, if any, distinguishing features. Or else other well-known fictional characters were imitated; there is one such instance, during the years when Edgar Rice Burroughs' 'Tarzan of the Apes' became a cult figure, when a publisher launched a similar series entitled 'Azan the Apeman'. No subtlety was used, no attempt made to disguise the fact that the copycat books were a deliberate 'rip-off'. As a result Edgar Rice Burroughs Inc. resorted to litigation and Azan disappeared from the book-stalls. It is interesting to note, though, that nowadays those Azan books have become much sought after collectors' items.

A lesson is there to be learned, though. Don't base your characters so obviously on somebody else's. In fact, it is better not to be influenced by other fictional characters because the copy will always live in the shadow of the original. Create your own!

Some of the pulps, described in Chapter 1, did create characters that lasted. 'The Shadow' is one that springs instantly to mind; Walter Brown Gibson (Maxwell Grant) was a prolific writer during the 'pulp era'. He was commissioned to write novels featuring 'The Shadow', who was already popular on radio in America in the 1930s. His first book was *The Living Shadow* (1934). Maxwell went on to write innumerable paperbacks about the masked figure of death striking down criminals, as many as 24 books a year. 'The Shadow' was also featured in a pulp magazine, comics and annuals. A blockbuster film *The Shadow* was released in 1994. Thus, a character created today may well become famous half a century hence.

Your characters are as important as your idea and your plot, make no mistake about that. As I have already mentioned, the 'Man in the Black Fedora' featured in two novels, without him there would have been none at all. *The Cadaver* would not have existed but for my nightmares.

Good characterization gives a novel credibility; poor characterization can detract from an excellent plot, no matter how well your book is written. The reader must be made to feel that he knows the characters personally, that if he saw one across the street tomorrow he would recognize him. Your aim must be to generate sympathy/hatred for the people you create; you must try to play on the emotions of your readership.

Obviously, the characters must fit the plot and respond accordingly. Having worked out your storyline, try to imagine what kind of people fit into it naturally, whether your main character is to be male or female, and from what walk of life.

Readers like to identify with characters so it is a good idea to make your heroes or heroines ordinary people. 'The Man in the Black Fedora' could not possibly be anything other than what he was, he is an exception to the rule, but if you look at many of my other novels you will note that the characters come from settings and situations which we all know. That way we can empathize with them.

In horror fiction generally, the early novels concentrated mostly on middle or upper class characters, principally because in those days it was basically only people from those classes who read books. It was necessary then, as it is nowadays, for the reader to identify with the people in the stories; today, readers come from all walks of life.

There is no hard and fast rule, the writer must have a 'feel' for his characters, and if he is comfortable with them then in all probability he has got it right.

So how does one go about creating the right kind of characters to suit a particular book? It depends upon the type of horror you are writing. Pulp-type horror does not generally feature intellectuals except maybe for a scientist to create or destroy some hideous monster. Psychological books are generally interwoven with more sophisticated people. These categories are by no means absolute, they are just to give you an idea.

Characters from scratch

Creating characters from scratch is both difficult and uncertain. They need characteristics and idiosyncrasies. Can you create these with credibility? If so, fine. You deserve to be a published author. Sometimes, though, this has to be done with the minor characters in your book. Perhaps you introduce somebody fleetingly in a chapter, someone who may not appear again, a bartender in a pub where your hero has just called in, possibly he has just arrived at the village where all the horrors have taken place. Even then, don't stereotype your bartender, and don't just pass him off as a nonentity. One little bit of detail here will add authenticity to your book. For example:

> A well built man limped from a doorway behind the bar, steadied himself against the counter, regarded the stranger briefly, then lowered his gaze. 'Can I help you?' He cleared his throat, looked away as he spoke.

A picture has been created in those few sentences of a man with some deformity and who is clearly nervous, perhaps fearful. Far better to describe him and his physical handicap briefly, incorporating some hint of fear, than to give a detailed physical description and state that the man seemed afraid of something. Let us suppose that the leading character has come to the village to investigate some strange happenings that have terrified the locals. The landlord of the pub is an ideal subject to mirror the fear experienced by his customers. Possibly he does not wish to discuss it with a stranger but by describing the meeting thus you have conveyed in a subtle way that there is something amiss around here. If that character is shown just once then enough has been written to interest the reader.

Charles Dickens was a master at creating characters. In this example we will look at one which he built up in a little known supernatural story *The Haunted Man and the Ghost's Bargain*:

> Who could have observed his manner - taciturn, thoughtful, gloomy, shadowed by habitual reserve, retiring always and jocund never, with a distraught air of reverting to a bygone place and time, or of listening to some old echoes in his mind - but might have said it was the manner of a haunted man? - who had seen him then, his work done, and he pondering in his chair before the rusted grate and red flame, moving his thin mouth as if in speech, but silent as the dead, would not have said that the man seemed haunted, and the chamber too?

This, surely, is a classical characterization that creates a 'haunted man'.

Likewise, minor characters should have mannerisms that are incorporated into any dialogue. It allows the reader to visualize a person, perhaps in his own imagination, identify with somebody he knows. In this way credibility is added to the story because 'real' people are being created rather than faceless figures. For example,

Harry Clements' eccentricities had become obsessions as adolescence merged into manhood. A doctor had once diagnosed his compulsion with having everything in neat piles or straight lines as 'symmetrical neurosis', an illness which had turned him into a recluse and set him apart from his fellow men, made him the subject of their ridicule although he was totally impervious to the remarks of those around him.

Here we have a mannerism, albeit an obsession, which is all part of a character build up. As the book unfolds (*Mania* by Guy N. Smith) many other eccentricities are added to Harry Clements' obsession with having everything in neat piles. His near-emaciated body giving him rounded shoulders and a shuffling, unsteady walk, his 'ration' of two cigarettes a day, the way he divides his evening meal into two halves and takes one back up to his room to eat later. We have a picture, not just of an eccentric, but of a miser.

Base your characters on real people

The best way of building up a character for your book is by basing him or her on somebody you know. This can be dangerous if you make the character too recognizable, particularly if he is the villain of the story. The easiest way round this is to change a few mannerisms and give a different physical description from that of your acquaintance. Mannerisms and idiosyncrasies are sometimes quite difficult to invent from cold.

You can describe a character quite differently from his or her appearance in real life but, in the actual writing of the book, they are that person as far as you are concerned. This often makes writing much easier and adds an extra dimension for the author. Somebody you dislike can meet a sticky end and only you will know about it! I 'collect' people's idiosyncrasies! One comes across so many in a variety of situations that, for a writer, it is wasteful to ignore them. You can observe people and their habits anywhere; in restaurants, on trains and buses, almost everywhere in public life. I make notes of what I observe, otherwise they are soon forgotten, and I know that a mixture of strange habits will all be put to good use eventually.

Some years ago we used to have a business associate who sometimes came to stay for a few days; his lifestyle was eccentric in the extreme. By the third day on one particular stay he was driving my wife and myself to distraction. He seemed oblivious of the family life that went on all around him and he used to come into my office and expound at great length on my working routine, how it could be changed for the better, and all manner of trivialities concerning himself. In addition, he had many, many strange and very annoying habits.

As I have stated, he seemed totally unaware of whatever I was doing and, in order to keep my sanity, I decided to treat him as a research subject. I put a sheet of paper in the typewriter and, during his constant chattering aand distractions, I typed out a comprehensive list of his eccentricities. He had no idea what I was doing. In fact, without the use of his magnifying glass he would have been unable to read it, anyway!

All of the material I gathered that day was used at some time or other in a number of books, spread amongst a variety of characters. They certainly brought my characters to life!

There are people who want to believe that they have been used as a character in an author's book. Likewise, there are those who are almost phobic in case they have been portrayed in a work of fiction. They will study every sentence of the printed pages, maybe even convince themselves that a certain character is based on themselves even if it is not the case. Where I have used real places as settings for my novels, people have asked me, hoping for a reply in the affirmative, 'That is *me* in the book, isn't it?' or, 'That isn't *me*, is it?' I never give a definite 'yes' to the former, it is always best to play safe. It may well not be them but if they choose to think it is, fair enough. The latter clearly do not want to be portrayed in a novel, so I reassure them accordingly.

Take a middle course, a mixture of people you know combined with various characteristics which you have picked up from various sources. You don't have to give a detailed physical description of a character, just a framework for the reader to build upon. All my life I have compiled my own image of fictional characters in the books I've read. All too often when I've gone to see a film of a book my conception of a favourite character has been ruined. Much of the pleasure derived from reading is in using your imagination alongside whatever the writer tells you. Give a good description of important physical features and leave the rest to the reader.

Limit the number of characters in your book. If you introduce too many characters who do not play an important role in the story, then the novel becomes confusing for both writer and reader; neither of you will be able to remember who is who and who has done what.

The setting of your book is a guide to what type of characters to use and how they will behave. If it is a down-trodden area of a town then middle class residents will be totally out of place. In a rural area you will expect to find farmers and country dwellers. Dialogue must be used accordingly.

Whatever your setting, it is best if you familiarize yourself with a similar area. Go and spend time in the country or downtown. Note the type of people you see, how they dress and speak. These are the characters you will need to use in your book.

Don't make people act out of character and try to avoid stereotypes; everybody is different, even in books. Don't go for what you consider to be the obvious just because you have read it elsewhere. Females do not always become hysterical, males do not always charge to the rescue of a damsel in distress, heedless of their own danger. Try to strike a balance.

Basing a character on yourself

Of course, you can always base a character on yourself. I have done this on more than one occasion. My first book *Werewolf by Moonlight* is set in the area in which we now live and which, prior to our move, I visited most weekends. So the leading character just had to be the tenant who visited at weekends for shooting! He fitted the storyline and the setting fitted him. In a scattered community such as this, where everybody knows everybody else, it was the safest bet; nobody could accuse me of basing Gordon Hall on any of the locals.

You can have a lot of fun basing a character on yourself and it will also make the writing of the book that much easier. You won't have any difficulty thinking up idioms and neither will you run the risk of offending anybody. It is a good opportunity for a self-analysis! And you can allow your ego to run riot!

To a lesser extent I based my 'Sabat' series on myself. I wrote Sabat's CV at the beginning of one of the books and used my own.

Series characters

I would advise the beginner to keep a file on each character from the very beginning. Note every detail, physical appearance, habits, eccentricities, age, any relatives' names. It will save a lot of time during the writing of the book as you will not have to keep looking back to check on a reference to a particular detail.

Also, there is a possibility that you might use the same character(s) in a future book. If you become a successful writer then there could be a follow-up book to your first one or it may even develop into a series.

Where a series is concerned, having a file on each character is essential. You can easily make a mistake which a reader will pick up, maybe even write in to the press and destroy the credibility of your series.

Do not forget to update the file. If you kill off a character, mark the reference clearly. Characters returning from the grave unintentionally are an acute embarrassment! If one marries, record whom he or she weds and when. Time sequences and relationships are an integral part of any series and they can become quite complicated in a long-running one.

Adopt a methodical approach to your characterization right from the very beginning.

Political correctness

There are no hard and fast rules concerning 'political correctness'. I don't really understand it and I doubt whether many other people do. It is so open to individual interpretation.

The essence of it all is not to cause offence to anybody, but in many cases it has been taken to the extreme and that which we used to take for granted in the past has become unacceptable to some sections of society who are looking to protest at anything and everything.

I once had to change the sex of a dog in one of my children's books simply to 'maintain a balance of the sexes'. On another occasion I was asked to make an elderly male vet female. Overall, it made not one jot of difference to the story, it simply created unnecessary work. In this latter case I had to create a new character which meant going back to the early part of the novel where the vet first appeared and ensuring that every 'he' became a 'she'. Where possible it is best to try to maintain a balance of the sexes throughout the book but the writer must ensure that the characters slot naturally into the narrative.

It all becomes very difficult if your novel happens to be set in the past. Characters must behave in books as they would be expected to do in real life, so a novel set before political correctness reared its head can present difficulties if you submit it to a publisher whose editor is a political correctness supporter.

It seems that you are walking on eggshells whatever you write and a book might be rejected simply because you have, in all innocence, offended a publisher. Unfortunately, there are no guidelines laid down and using your commonsense is not always the answer. All I can advise is that you ensure, to the best of your knowledge that there is nothing blatantly racist, sexist, ageist or any other 'ist' you can think of. You will have to be prepared to carry out revisions and pander to seemingly pointless suggestions. Otherwise you will not be published.

Policical correctness poses more problems in the creation of characters than it does in the writing of a story. In the text you can avoid anything that might be offensive but in a real world there are people who are definitely 'ists', and you cannot pretend that they do not exist. Your characters should evolve from the plot, background and location (eg inner city). You must not try to make them something they are not merely to comply with political correctness. On the other hand, do not highlight anything that might be considered offensive just for the sake of it. There are good and bad people all around us; they are there to be written about.

If you create the right characters for your novel then that is a major step towards publication.

4

The plot

You have expanded your idea, you have created your characters around it, and now you have to work these into a detailed credible plot. At the outset, though, you have to have a 'feel' for everything that you have done so far; if you don't really like your characters or you are not really inspired by the idea, then what follows from hereon will not make much impact. If you become bored with the book, then that will be passed on to the editor who reads it. You have to convince yourself that this is a book which people will read avidly; without that motivation you may as well go back to the beginning and start looking for another idea and creating new characters. Don't delude yourself. If you are not sure it is right, begin again. It is frustrating but it is preferable to get it right at the beginning.

At this stage you should know into which horror category your novel is going to slot. Roughly there are four types of horror novel and you will need to write your book with your prospective readership in mind:

1. basic horror ie straightforward beasts on the rampage, pulp-style, simplistic stories,

2. the occult (witchcraft and black magic),

3. psychological horror which has a wide scope and may span both the horror and crime fiction genres. *The Silence of the Lambs* did this to great effect, although I prefer to categorize serial killer books as police procedural novels,

4. others. Again, the dividing line between crime fiction, science fiction and horror is a debatable one. Your fiction may even be based on true-life horror.

These are merely guidelines to give you some idea of the market at which you are aiming. The narrative is a priority from now on.

An idea on its own is not a plot, it is merely a starting point on which you must build. There is a common belief that a book has to be divided into three sections: the beginning, the middle and the end and that things go from bad to worse until finally everything comes right. That was fine for books written thirty or forty years ago, but today's readers do not like predictability. Nowadays you need to have a beginning but where you go from there is entirely up to you. Agreed, the book must end sometime but it does not necessarily have to come to a definite conclusion. Good does not necessarily have to triumph over evil and make everything nice and cosy. You could try letting the baddies win for once. If the reader is disappointed he will remember the book; at least if you generate frustration it means the reader sympathizes with the characters.

But whatever you decide upon, your book must be thoroughly thought out before you even pick up the pen or begin tapping on the keyboard otherwise you will create all kinds of problems for yourself. Make a start with those characters you have created, type out a list of names and alongside them list what they look like, how old they are and any mannerisms they have. At this stage you will only be able to compile the major characters, minor ones will materialize as you continue writing. Add them to your list, too; you never know when they will appear again. It all saves time.

Now you are ready to slot the characters into a plot.

Type out a synopsis of your book in as much detail as possible at this stage. I always compile mine chapter by chapter as this enables me to 'pace' the book; you do not want to discover that you have used up the bulk of your storyline in the first few chapters. Neither do you want to over-write as this tends to make a book very 'padded'. If you realize that you are doing this, you must look back on what you have written. A beginner is sometimes apt to go into too much irrelevant detail; you don't need a detailed account of a character's journey from A to B if nothing of interest has happened en route. It is sufficient to mention that he arrived at his destination by bus/train/car, or even to continue the narrative once he is there.

Aim to cover around twenty chapters in your initial story outline. You will find that during the course of writing, one chapter runs to two or, alternatively, two proposed chapters can be covered in one. You do not have to stick rigidly to your chapter breakdown, you must be flexible.

There is no guidance as to chapter wordage. Some are longer than others, they should end naturally, either on a cliffhanger or when a particular episode is concluded (for the moment). But in plotting a book of 20 chapters, very roughly look at each chapter being 4000–5000 words in length. That will help you to pace the finished book.

You will be surprised how the compilation of a synopsis enables you to expand your original storyline. As the story unfolds, you will think of additional happenings. An editor once told me that I submit the most detailed synopses which she has ever received, mostly writers send in a couple of pages of a basic storyline in the hope of receiving a commission to write their book. I like to know exactly where I am going when I type Chapter One; invariably, I make changes as I go along but it is a comfort to know that I have the entire plot to refer to. I know that I won't run dry!

Some experienced authors just let an idea roll, unfold as it goes. They delight in how it all turns out just as if they were reading somebody else's book. I prefer to know what is going to happen - I can always change it if I want to.

I believe a synopsis is essential. I always compile one whether I am seeking a commission or writing a book straight off.

Research

Now is the time to research any aspects of which you are not certain relating to your proposed book. Far better to do some research now than later; there could just be something which destroys the credibility of your story which might have saved a lot of writing time if only you had discovered it before you began writing. For instance, some chemical, or whatever, responsible for the ecological disaster you are writing about might prove to be relatively harmless in the situation you have painstakingly developed. It is preferable to ensure that technicalities work and do what you want them to do.

If your book is set in a particular locality, visit that place, take some photographs and generally get the feel of the area. Collect as much trivia relating to the surrounding locality as possible: guide books and leaflets, train and bus timetables, a street map etc. They will all help to ensure that you get your basic facts right.

Attention to detail is vital, only then will your book be convincing. If one of your characters uses a gun then state, without the information appearing to have come direct from a firearms manual, the type of weapon he uses. If an automatic pistol holds a clip of fifteen bullets, then to have him firing off twenty without reloading is nonsense. Some weaponry expert is almost sure to spot your faux pas. Quote models of guns and vehicles used by your characters; brand names are much used in novels since Stephen King started the trend. But you have to get your facts right. It does add to that necessary atmosphere of authenticity.

I have already mentioned my scrapbook method of amassing research material but that is something which happens over a long period of time; it has taken me years to build up a library of newspaper clippings. You could always start now, though, looking ahead to writing more books in the future. In the meantime you will need to use a public library.

Use your synopsis as a guide to your research requirements, and utilize your library visit to its maximum potential. Research must be a methodical procedure; use a notebook and jot down every bit of information that might come in useful. There is nothing more annoying than starting to write, after a lengthy session of compiling facts away from home, and then to discover that there is something which you omitted to note at the time. A false start is both time-wasting and demoralizing.

Make copious notes and if there is anything you are unsure about, now is the time to sort it out. You will find, just as you did in the compilation of your synopsis, that one thing leads to another. Whenever you find cross-references, follow them up. It is better to come away with more material than you need, than just a few sketchy notes.

There are no strict guidelines to research except to find out as much as possible about the subject on which you are going to write a book. The temptation is to over-research, ie compile notebooks full of irrelevant information. In the beginning compile what you consider to be important data that will be relevant to your book. The other pitfall, when writing your book, is to think that you have to use up every bit of research you have painstakingly gleaned. If you do that then your book will read like a reference work. Your aim is to be able to write with authority about something round which your plot revolves without appearing to show off a superior knowledge. Research should blend naturally into your text.

However thorough you have been, it is doubtful whether one visit to the library will be enough. Return if you need to, never rely on guesswork. There is always some reader out there eager to prove you wrong. And if you are fortunate enough to receive reviews, reviewers are mercilessly scathing in their comments.

Get it right first time!

Subplots

If you are going to work a subplot into your book, the time to map it out is now. It has to slot naturally into the storyline as a means of both increasing tension and bringing short-lived light relief from the terrible events you are relating in your horror novel. It either has to be done properly or not at all.

I have some reservations about subplots. In some books I have read it is blatantly obvious that they have been inserted either as an afterthought or on editorial insistence. If those subplot pages were extracted they could be bound up into a separate novel that bore little relation to the one from which they have been extracted. I suspect that the publishers have decided that the original work lacked length and the writer has increased the number of pages by integrating a subplot at the ratio of a few pages in every chapter. The text will not flow and will be jerky to the reader.

These contrived subplots stand out like the proverbial sore thumb. Currently, huge tomes are in vogue on the bestseller stands and the principle seems to be that the bigger the book, the better it will sell because buyers think that they are getting more for their money. It all comes back to my aforementioned advice on overwriting, only in this case it is a deliberate ploy.

If you think that a subplot will enhance your book, then think long and hard about it, how to use it and where in the novel. It needs to be relative to the main plot and must merge with it in due course. The stereotyped subplot is one where the lead character's partner is having an extra-marital affair and in due course the 'other' man, or woman, becomes embroiled in the main plot.

Unless you are able to link plot and subplot credibly then all you are doing is combining two separate novels. Again characterization is important; strong characters are vital if a subplot is to work.

I remember an editor once talking to me about what made an 'international' bestseller. He told me that the book needed to be complicated. I don't agree; I have always favoured simplicity, whatever the length or subject matter of a book. The best authors write simply, using good English to their advantage. Admittedly, modern espionage novels that contain a certain amount of technical information can seem complicated but there is a way of weaving that technology into a straightforward thriller. Fortunately, very few horror novels are technical apart from the 'Back to the Future-type' plot and, personally, I would categorize that as science fiction. Horror writers should have a basic knowledge of police procedure, though, particularly if they write in my third category of horror plot described at the beginning of this chapter.

As already mentioned, police procedure can be accumulated 'on file' by building up a scrapbook from newspapers. Often the police themselves will be most helpful in this matter; they don't want incorrect procedures written in books. Any specific queries will almost always be answered in a visit to your local police station. A personal visit is preferable to a phone call. And, of course, there are always books available at the library, but make sure that they are up to date.

Remember, you are writing for people who read for pleasure and you must produce a good story that is well told. A mass of technical information gleaned from the library must not be used to 'write down' to your readership. Readers are often much more clever than writers, this shallow attempt at intellectuality will be only too transparent.

Include your proposed subplot in your synopsis. Write a couple of chapters of your novel and then you should be in a position to decide if your secondary storyline fits or whether it is really needed at all.

Violence

I think it is preferable if the matter of violence in your novel is decided at synopsis stage. You have built up your characters and storyline; violence should only be used where it falls naturally into the story and suits the characters. If it is used gratuitously, it will stand out plainly as contrived. Do not use it to make up a shortfall in wordage if you find yourself under-writing.

A horror novel does not necessarily have to have any violence in it, particularly one where the theme is that of psychological terror. In this case, violence would destroy the credibility of a plot that focuses on the workings of the mind.

Violence in the basic horror novel is acceptable but even then it need not be described in every gory detail. My 'Crabs' series are packed with violence but I think this is acceptable because the crustaceans themselves are of a fantasy nature. Crabs as big as cows are unlikely to crawl out of the ocean and begin mutilating mankind. So it is a fantasy situation; mutilations are expected when Man meets monster. But should my invading army have been one of psychopaths rather than crabs, the blood and gore would have been distasteful.

The gruesome parts in *The Silence of the Lambs* were cleverly done. You heard about the serial killer's mutilations secondhand, ie dialogue between police officers and the chilling psychoanalysis of the cannibal. Nowhere is the act of flaying a human being recounted as it happened. In this way, probably the most bizarre and gory violence ever to be written is presented in a manner that lifts this novel above books of a similar nature. Read it and see what I mean.

Obviously this device cannot be employed in all books about serial killers but often the horror which is not described is far more frightening to the reader. Upon the discovery of a mutilated corpse. . .

> The officer fought the urge to throw up, forced himself to view the mutilation because it was his duty. The open throat grinned up at him. He had to turn away, get himself back under control before he radioed for backup.

That is a gruesome passage, but an awful lot more could have been described in detail. Who really wants to know? Isn't that enough? The reader's imagination will create all that you have left out and this is one of the advantages the written story has over the visual. The reader will see what he wants to see. Implication is always preferable, subtlety has a greater impact than a gory passage. And, if you like, you can describe the mutilations in a documented manner in a later conversation between pathologist and police officer.

Violence is different from horror. The former sickens, the latter frightens. The icy touch on the back of the neck on a dark night is terrifying, the bloodied mutilated body is revolting. Graphic carnage is best avoided or not described in full, mutilation must have a reason that fits the story. Those horror books of the early 1970s are a couple of decades out of fashion.

In defence of violence in books, I do not accept the media's claims that violent books create violent people. Violent criminals have had a violent disposition long before they began reading about it in books. If they read at all.

Sex

Likewise, erotic books do not turn men into rapists. Just the reverse, in my opinion. Nevertheless, there are few novels, horror or otherwise, which do not have some sexual content these days and it is as well that the writer becomes familiar with the various ways in which it is portrayed.

The more subtle the sex scenes, the greater turn-ons they become. Sex should come naturally in a book, the writer should not even contemplate putting it into his synopsis. However, this is as good a place as any to discuss it.

Contrived sex is as obvious as gratuitous violence to the reader. There are no hard and fast rules concerning whether or not adult books should contain sex. It should depend upon the relationship that exists between two people in the story. Sex at first sight does not ring true.

Situations will develop and the writer should weigh up whether or not to portray a couple in a sex scene and, if so, how to describe it. Terror is not conducive to sex so a man and woman trapped in a haunted building throughout the nocturnal hours would be most unlikely to copulate. But a couple, perhaps portrayed in the sub-plot, and away from the escalating horrors enshrouding the main characters would, in all probability, make love.

Occult themes are heavy with sexual implications; most black magic rites are sexually influenced, there will be orgies rather than a gentle lead up to the act. So the writer must determine how to handle this aspect or else his book will have pornographic overtones.

Portray the scene, the nudity, the frenzied escalation of lust, describe it through the eyes of whichever of your characters is involved. The climax to such a scene might read:

> The night atmosphere was heavy with the odour from cavorting bodies, the circle began to close. Now they were close, brushing, touching, stroking whichever of the opposite sex was nearest to them. Moans as searching fingers found that which they were seeking. And then this mass of lusting humanity fell, writhing and kicking as their ultimate desires were fulfilled. Finally, it was all over and the coven lay in an exhausted heap, spent and quivering.

Note that there are no graphic descriptions, no mention of sexual organs. It has all happened, the reader has visualized it. On this occasion he does not need to have the details explained to him. In fact, it would spoil a few moments of erotic reading for him if the author described any part of the climax of this satanic mass.

Then, snatch it away from him, plunge him back into an atmosphere of terror. Perhaps some entity materializes, answers the call of evil.

Without sex this gathering of devil worshippers would have lacked reality. The writer has done enough; now, on with the main plot.

The advice given in this chapter is, of course, my own method of preparation for writing a book. Doubtless other writers prepare in a variety of different ways. All I can say is that my way has stood me in good stead for the many books which I have written and had published so I see no reason to alter it. But whatever mode of preparation you feel most comfortable with, it must be well organized. That will put you one rung up the ladder to success.

Having completed your synopsis, read it through and put it away for a few days. Think about it; have you anything else to add? Or to take away? Are you satisfied that your research has been thorough enough for you to begin writing your novel?

Imagine the detailed storyline as a full-length book, and ask yourself one final question: if you had bought that book, written by another author, would it have appealed to you? That must be your criterion. If the answer is 'yes' then it is time to begin writing.

5

Start writing

Making a start

Now that all the preparation has been done, you are finally ready to make a start. Understandably, the first-time writer will be filled with trepidation. This is the crunch, can you really do it? There is only one way to find out. I have spoken with many people who are 'always going to write a book'. They have what seems to me to be quite a good idea to work on but they never ever get around to taking that decisive step. Why? Simply because they are frightened that they might discover that they cannot do it; they are afraid to come face–to–face with defeat.

It isn't as bad as you think. You can always rewrite, try again, and it is not something which has to be completed at one sitting. You will not know whether you have been successful for a very long time, anyway. Indeed, some manuscripts have gathered dust for years until, out of the blue on a belated impulsive submission, a publisher has accepted them. Some bestsellers, written by household names, have gone the rounds of publishing houses and the author has abandoned all hopes of ever seeing his work in print. And then one day, it has happened.

But it cannot happen until you write your book.

Word processor? typewriter? by hand?

I used to write by hand simply because I had a job that allowed me time to write whilst I was at work; I wrote in exercise books and paid a typist to type up my output to avoid duplicating work at home. Then when I became a full-time professional writer I used a manual Imperial 66 typewriter (I still have that same machine and find it invaluable for correspondence without disturbing the book which I am working at on the word processor). In those days word processors (WPs) were not even dreamt of and when they first came on the market they were far too expensive to buy, anyway.

I well remember buying my first Amstrad PCW 8512. Other writers were extolling the virtues of the word processor so I decided to give it a try. That took as much courage as starting to write a first book! My children were brought up with computers at school but for me it was an alien world. I plucked up the courage, walked into a computer shop and told the assistant that if she would teach me the basics in a way that I could understand, I would buy a machine. She was most helpful; several hours later I had the WP back home and I have never looked back since. Five years on I am told that my Amstrad is obsolete but I still use it.

One word of advice concerning word processors if you are new to them. A retailer will thrust a tome of a manual at you and tell you that 'it's all in there, everything you need to know'. He or she is right but, if you have no previous knowledge of WPs then the information within that book will be a mass of incomprehensible terminology. If you have a friend who is reasonably conversant with the computer world, ask them to spare you some time. Prepare your own manual, in simple language, of just the options that you will need to use.

Computer buffs are generally only too delighted to show off their expertise; they will want to demonstrate how to do all kinds of weird and wonderful things that bear no relation to writing a horror novel. This will only confuse you. My own 'self-help manual', compiled with the help of my eldest daughter, tells me everything that I need to know from setting the WP up for writing to printing out my finished and edited work. That is quite sufficient for me.

The WP has just about everything going for it; you can edit as you go along which saves the laborious task of writing a second draft. As a result you can produce virtually word perfect manuscripts, and you have the discs to refer to if any revision needs to be done at a later stage. But, of course, there are snags. . . like the time I hit a 'purple patch' and was working so fast that I neglected to 'save and continue'; 3000 words and several hours later, we had a mini power failure, just a flickering of the lights, and it was enough to lose everything I had written. I rewrote the lot! And there is always the risk of getting an 'error in the disc', a fault with the software that prevents you either from printing out or extracting the work you have completed. That has happened to me on a couple of occasions.

Nowadays many publishers request that books are submitted on disc. It gives me an uneasy feeling; suppose for some reason my software was not compatible with theirs, or an error had crept into the disc. Or some other terrible snag that has not even occurred to me. But it is a sign of the times and we must not resist progress. The safest way is to print out the manuscript as usual and then submit the disc with it.

It is all a question of writing by whichever means you are comfortable using. Many of today's big name writers still use a ballpoint. It really doesn't matter; it is the finished product that counts. If your publisher insists on having your work on disc, and you are really unable to master a WP, then you will have no alternative but to pay somebody to put it on disc for you. And that will prove quite expensive.

Page layout

It is useful to establish a formula for the presentation of a manuscript. A good novel may well be rejected because of single-spacing, narrow margins or anything else that makes it difficult to read. You must produce a manuscript that looks professional and is easy on the eye; that is step one in putting the reader in the right frame of mind.

A4 is the standard size paper used with either WPs or typewriters. The ideal layout is to allow 25 lines per page with 10 words to the line. This gives ample margins for editing, and it also enables you to work out quite easily how many words approximately you have completed as you go along. A line counts as 10 words even if it consists only of a short sentence or a single word of dialogue. So when you have completed your first four pages you will know that you have written approximately a thousand words. Your 100,000-word novel should run to 400 pages of manuscript.

Do not attempt to pad out your work by including incessant short dialogue. That was a ploy used by some writers in the pulp magazines in the 1930s. And who can really blame them when they were working on a pittance of one cent a word! Some of the regular series contained a lengthy introductory synopsis of the character and how he came to exist and what had gone before. Often the writers were paid for this résumé which in some ways compensated for their low rate of pay. However, this does not happen today and, particularly with a book, repetition is to be avoided.

Never staple or clip the chapters together. A completed manuscript can be submitted with a rubber band round it to hold the pages together. For years I have submitted mine in a polythene freezer bag; it looks better and keeps the pages clean. Manuscripts in folders are something which we shall discuss in the next chapter.

I mention the submission of manuscripts here simply to prevent the novice writer from becoming over-zealous with a stapler and spoiling the presentation. Presentation counts for a lot before an editor even looks at what you have written.

The title page should contain your name and address and an approximation of the wordage of the book.

Begin each chapter on a new sheet about a quarter of the way down. Just think, you've written about 65 words before you even start! A trick used by those legendary pulp writers was to start a fresh chapter about halfway down the page and end each chapter near to the top of a page. Some writers boasted that in this way they were paid for stories, over a number of years, which they had never written! I would not advocate this, though, because a book written like this takes on an 'empty' look which will at once be apparent to the editor and you may well have ruined a cliffhanger at the end of a chapter by cutting it down to a few words.

Let your style and writing roll, give it a free rein and do not even think about how many words you have written. Only consider wordage at stages throughout the book when you refer to your synopsis to check whether you might be underwriting or overwriting.

Self-discipline

I consider self-discipline to be an important factor which will determine whether or not a beginner makes a career out of writing. It is all too often neglected in advice to writers and I make no apology for discussing it at some length.

You need to set yourself a target, without it you will not have a daily or weekly goal to reach and 'tomorrow' has an unhealthy appeal. Certainly at the outset your writing schedule needs to be a very modest one; at this stage you have no idea what your output will be and you could be putting yourself under unnecessary pressure by aiming too high.

Unless you start with a methodical approach you could join the ranks of the well-intentioned people who are always going to write a book. The only difference will be that yours has already been started. It might never be completed.

If you have a full-time job, and if there will be evenings and weekends when you are unable to write at all, set yourself a target of 5000 words a week. If you find that too much, reduce it to whatever you can manage comfortably. Only *you* know what you can achieve.

Even now, after 100 books, I still schedule my work; my target is

10,000 words a week. Sometimes I exceed, sometimes I fall below it due to unforeseen distractions and family pressures, but if that happens then I am not unduly concerned because I will generally be slightly ahead of schedule. If for a couple of weeks I manage to write 15,000 words then I have a week in hand. Getting behind with your schedule puts pressure on you; you are tempted to rush and rushed writing isn't good writing.

But in the beginning there is no pressure. You are writing a book which you hope to sell; it is not a commissioned book with a deadline for the delivery of the manuscript. Your priority should be to produce quality work, a week or two extra is of no consequence with regard to completion. All the same, do not lapse into apathy. You need to finish your book within a reasonable time.

If you are successful in becoming a full-time writer then it is likely that your future books will be commissioned, and that is when the pressure really begins. At the moment you are experimenting, you will know by the time you have completed your first novel what your average weekly output is. You will find that your writing speed increases without your making any conscious effort to write faster. Indeed, I would urge you not to attempt this consciously. Likewise, each book you write will be better than your last one. This comes from experience.

Editors have different ideas on how quickly a book should be written. I have worked with some who commissioned 4-book contracts and were more than delighted to have a typescript delivered in advance of the contractual delivery date. Others urged me to take my time: 'There's no rush, we can always allow an extra week or two.' Basically, the latter editors feel that anything written quickly will be of poor quality. Whilst their intentions are sound, it is neither practical nor morale-boosting to know that deadlines are not rigid. A professional has to earn a living; whether the book is written in ten or fifteen weeks will make no difference to its quality but by taking longer he or she will not have increased their earnings. As an employee, you could not afford to forego five weeks' wages. Comparing writing with a regular wage-earning job puts this point into perspective.

Ideally, a professional writer is, by scheduling his work and keeping to deadlines, hopefully budgeting for a living wage. Your aim, though, is for good sales with royalties earned in the future.

The golden rule should be never to tell editors how long it takes you to write a book. You can always defer delivery of the manuscript until the contractual date, if necessary, and proceed with other commissions in the meantime.

Thus, having decided upon your working schedule, the most important thing is to keep to it. If you have completed your weekly quote by, say, Thursday, then it is permissible to take Friday off if you really need to. Otherwise, allow yourself the luxury of getting a day ahead and use that day in hand for something that crops up.

Decide when and for how long you are going to write. As you are probably restricted to part-time writing, do not overload your programme. Writing needs to be a pleasure, a hobby at this stage. The last thing you want is to become bored with it, so you need to make time for relaxation; your writing will benefit from it.

Determine whether you are a 'morning' or an 'evening' person. Even though you may have no choice concerning which part of the day you devote to writing, it could well be that you turn out your best work before midday, which means that your weekends will be invaluable to you. It is all a matter of individual preference; what is important is getting the writing done.

Liken your first attempt at writing a book to a training course in which you need to qualify at the end, to attain a certain standard. You will almost certainly fail on 'poor attendance'.

Authors should provide quality work, but editors also want an author who delivers their manuscript on time and who is easy to work with.

Starting your book

I always compare writing a book with embarking upon a long train journey. The train may stop, you eat, rest and sleep, but you do not disembark until you reach your journey's end. So it is with writing: you will be with your book until you have completed it.

Arguably, the first paragraph is the most important paragraph. It needs to arouse the interest of an editor so that he or she will read on, maybe then make you an offer for your work. The opening paragraph still has an important function, it must attract the attention of casual browsers in bookshops who hopefully, will then buy the book.

That paragraph needs to be punchy and well written, and, obviously, hint at horrors to come. I quote one of my own from *Witch Spell* (published by Zebra, New York, 1993):

> Yvonne Wheeler knew that somebody was following her. She
> had sensed a presence in the dimly lit side streets long before
> her ears picked up the sound of footsteps some way behind her,
> a fast tip-tapping in time with her own. It stopped when she

did, began again when she hurried on. Now her heartbeat was thudding with the steps like a muffled tomtom.

Who was it who was following Yvonne Wheeler down the dimly lit side streets? Why were they following her? What will happen to her?

I could well have begun the book in a boring fashion, described how Yvonne had left her house, what she was wearing and where she was heading. And who on earth would have wanted to know all that right at the start of a book? It would have destroyed completely the impact. Excite your readers, titillate their imaginations, even scare them in that first paragraph. Make them want to find out what happens and to do that they will have to buy the book!

But that pace and interest must be sustained and this is something which the novice must bear in mind. Don't use up all your best suspense in the opening pages and then let the book fall flat.

Application

Successful writing can be summed up in one word - application. It is the combination of an idea and a plot, and both have to be portrayed in a way that appeals to your proposed readership. You have your idea, you have worked out your plot and now I may be able to provide some help in writing it in book length form.

Dialogue

Dialogue is important in any novel. It has to be written as people speak in real life and how they would be expected to speak in given circumstances. Bad dialogue is as boring as text that waffles on without getting anywhere. Say what needs to be said; create tension where it is needed by terse dialogue. Nobody in the midst of a crisis would ramble on. Dialogue can be mastered from reading contemporary fiction. Do not be influenced by older books, even the horror classics mentioned earlier, because mostly that speech is melodramatic. Films are another source for mastering the art of dialogue.

Dialogue is useful in a number of ways; it can be used to build characterization; how characters speak, what they say and how they say it can often describe them much more fully than a paragraph of detailed description. It can also be a useful aid to the narrative. Suppose, as an example, an ecological disaster has destroyed a community and you need to communicate to your readership the full extent of the horror. Do it through a conversation between a couple of the survivors. In this way you can create a far more tense and horrifying situation than by simply cataloguing the events. You can convey the terror and despair of those still living and determine what action is being taken to stay alive. The following example is taken from my novel *The Knighton Vampires* published by Piatkus Books in 1993:

> 'What's that?'
> He saw her stiffen, her head turned towards the window. The curtain wafted, a summer draught had found a gap in the ill-fitting frame.
> 'It's just the breeze. These old windows . . . '
> 'I heard something, John!'
> 'Like I told you', he grasped her, his fingers pinched her smooth flesh in his irritation at this diversion, 'it's just the breeze. Up here there's always a breeze, even in the hottest weather.'
> 'No, it wasn't the wind.' She tried to sit up but his weight was pinning her down. 'It was like . . . somebody tapped on the window.'
> 'Night moths', he grunted.'Louder than that.'
> 'Well, I didn't hear anything.' He swung a flabby leg over her.
> 'John, please . . . go and look.'

Here the dialogue has been used to its fullest potential. She has heard something and her terror is just beginning. He has not heard anything and, anyway, he is too interested in having sex with her. The combination of fear and annoyance at the distraction provide conflict. She begs him to go and find out what has been tapping on the window.

Reluctantly, he goes to look. There is something nasty outside the window. Vampires, in fact. Now, had I simply described the arrival of those mythical undead visitors at this remote dwelling, I would have lost much impact. She is uneasy, starts to become frightened. What is out there? He finds out when he goes to look but the seeds have been sown for a scene of stark terror that becomes far more terrifying in its build-up through the dialogue of the amorous couple.

An exclamation mark can be used effectively for emphasis but don't overdo it or else it becomes exceedingly annoying to the reader and loses its impact.

Bad language

My advice is to keep bad language in dialogue to a minimum; use it only when it feels right. Your characters should determine this. Never use it simply to shock; it is doubtful whether bad language in books shocks anybody these days. If it is overused it is exceedingly irritating and becomes boring. However, it is necessary to use swear words in certain instances to add credibility to the characters in your story. It is a sign of the times. Rarely, before the 1960s, did one come across it. Except, of course, in *Lady Chatterley's Lover*. Once a court had ruled, on appeal, that the book was not obscene, the floodgates were opened.

I used bad language in some of my early horror books because it was expected. I had no choice. On more than one occasion an editor has requested me to use it. A useful criterion in determining how strong to make your dialogue lies in whether you intend your book for hardcover or original paperback publication. Nowadays your main outlet for hardcover fiction will be the libraries and libraries are less likely to take it if the pages are liberally sprinkled with bad language.

Whatever you do, do not use obscenities outside narrative. For preference, I would rather not use bad language at all but then I would fail in my attempts to create credible characters and situations in which they find themselves.

As with sex in your book, use swear words only where they crop up naturally because that is how it is in real life.

Humour

The occasional bit of humour, even in a horror novel, can bring light relief. But it must be original and funny; unfunny humour makes for an amateurish book. Dialogue is by far the best way to inject some light humour otherwise it needs to be very subtle.

'Blank spots'

I have heard other writers talk about 'writer's block' but, never having experienced unfortunate periods when words will not come and it becomes impossible to write at all, I cannot tell you much about it. However, from time to time, I do experience what I term 'blank spots'.

A 'blank spot' usually occurs after I have hit a 'purple patch' (a spell of writing that flows so well that I'm tapping the keyboard at a ferocious pace; the words come, the horror is at its most terrifying and the characters do everything that you could expect of them). If it lasted I would finish the book in about half the scheduled time and its quality would be the very best which I am able to produce. But along comes that dreaded 'blank spot'. . . I suddenly realize that I'm in a vacuum. It is only a temporary state; I'm more than satisfied with what has gone before and I know what is going to happen later on. But for the moment everything has slowed to a standstill.

This state has arisen due to a slowing down of events in my otherwise detailed synopsis. I've taken a small part of the book for granted, nothing much happens in it. The synopsis in question might read 'Haggard goes to the police station, discusses events with a senior officer, agrees to assist the police.' That sounded fine when I plotted it but I'm in danger of writing a chapter that will serve to bore the reader with dialogue that merely recaps previous happenings. The only real 'bones' in that proposed chapter is Haggard agreeing to help the police.

The way to get around this when it occurs is to go back to the synopsis, study what you have written to date and what is going to happen when you overcome the obstacle that has arisen. All right, Haggard needs to go to the police station and team up with the law but you need to inject something else that will keep up the pace and will not detract from the story.

That 'missing link' may be discovered in an unplanned scene, perhaps a further atrocity which leads to your character's visit to the police station. Handled right, it will increase the action and make for a better book. Contrived, it will stand out as sheer padding. But your synopsis will be the key to your solution.

Alternatively, it may be preferable to leave out this chapter, leapfrog Haggard's next move into the next chapter, and make it slightly longer and stronger. But check that by so doing you are not under-writing and, as a result, will finish up with a shortfall on your wordage.

Always keep a strict watch on your synopsis as you write. You are under no obligation to adhere to it; as your book unfolds changes may present themselves which will be of benefit. Do not hesitate to effect variations.

Completing your book

Just as that first paragraph may well be instrumental in the success of your book, so will your first book be an important factor in whether or not you progress to a second one. It has to be very good from start to finish; rewrite anything with which you are not satisfied but don't lose confidence to the extent that you find yourself rewriting for ever more.

Somebody once said to me that his trouble was that every single thing he wrote he then saw a need to rewrite again and again. It turned out that what he had written in the first place was, in fact, good enough. He just saw how it could be written in different ways. Take a sentence or paragraph from any book and there are a number of permutations in how those words could be rearranged or substituted so that their meaning is exactly the same. This man was indecisive by nature; had he seriously attempted to write a book then there would have been dozens of different versions of it over the next decade. He would never ever have been satisfied.

Eventually, the writer has to be confident enough to know when what he has written is as good as he is ever likely to make it. One must be of a positive frame of mind. Indecisive rewriting will only serve to destroy what was originally a good book.

Individual emotions vary upon the completion of a book. You will possibly experience euphoria after the long weeks of painstaking labour; maybe you will feel sadness because it is all over, and that is a very good sign that you have been totally committed throughout and become involved with your characters.

Inevitably you will have a sense of relief because you have achieved that which you set out to do. It's over now, you have done your very best, the die is cast, success or failure is in the lap of the gods.

I went through a period some years ago when I experienced a migraine the day after I finished each book. It became so predictable that I catered for it, ensured that there were no appointments in my diary for that date. Obviously the migraine was brought about by a long period of stress (writing is stressful, no matter how much one enjoys it), and the sudden termination of anxiety. I mentioned this to the family doctor once. He told me that you can never achieve anything worthwhile without taking something out of yourself. Never were truer words spoken!

Now that you have completed your book don't rush to mail it off to some publisher whose imprint you have seen in numbers on the shelves of your local bookshop. It is tempting to think that you might become an overnight millionaire but the chances are that you won't.

Put your manuscript away and don't read it through again. Foremost is your need to relax, to pursue another hobby for a week or so. It is no good advising you to forget all about your novel because that will be an impossibility but do try to stop thinking about it other than as a finished product. Otherwise you may well become like my acquaintance who rewrote and rewrote. Only when you are relaxed and have both feet firmly back on terra firma must you begin rereading.

Revising and rewriting

It is very difficult to read one's own work objectively and in an unbiased frame of mind but that is what you must do. Try to think of your manuscript as a book you have just bought and read it as you would a novel by another author. Do not even consider revision at this stage.

My wife is my best critic. She is an avid reader of books and she is honest in her opinions concerning my work. She does not just tell me what she thinks I want to hear. Most of the time her criticisms are valid, and that is an invaluable help to me.

If you have such a partner, that will help towards achieving your ambition to become a published author. If not, then you will have to rely upon your own judgment. Whatever you do, do not pass your manuscript round your friends for them to read; you will end up with all manner of conflicting advice and, if you are foolish enough to heed it and do some rewriting, your book will probably be damned from the outset.

Neither must you try to persuade a published author to read your work and to 'give an opinion'. He will doubtless decline, just as I would. Writers are too busy with their own books to undertake the reading of aspiring authors' work. Also, it is a dangerous practice to involve oneself with unpublished books. Coincidences cannot be ruled out; just suppose that that established author had an idea in embryo form, or even a completed yet still unpublished novel, which bore a similarity to one that he was asked to 'vet'. It could well cause embarrassment and unpleasantness in the future.

Read your own manuscript and make up your own mind; be positive and decisive. Do not be tempted to revise too heavily at this early stage but make notes of any aspects which you think might improve your book and think them through carefully.

Then, if you think some revision is necessary, get on with it. One aspect to look for is balance in a book. Every book should maintain an equilibrium; what you must avoid is a rush of action and plot development at the outset which dwindles away as the story progresses. Or, at the other extreme, nothing very much happening for a long time and then events all crammed together just as if you had only just thought of them. Your novel should be a developing story.

Eventually, though, there comes a time when you must finally settle for what you have written. After that you really must try to forget all about your novel as far as the writing of it is concerned; it must now become a unit which you are trying to sell, and you must channel all your efforts into finding a publisher for it.

Often that is harder than the writing of the book itself.

6

Finding a publisher

We have now reached the most important hurdle of all in our efforts to see your book in print - finding a publisher. You have laboured for weeks, probably months, and now you want to harvest the fruits of your efforts. Perhaps I may be forgiven for becoming pessimistic before I become optimistic, but I must emphasize that this is the hardest phase en route to publication. However, nothing worthwhile in life is easily achieved.

I have met people who, years after having written their first book, are still submitting it to publishers. I admire their perseverance but after so long one can only come to one of two conclusions: either the book is totally unpublishable or else they have been sending it to the wrong publishers.

One of the big drawbacks with submitting unsolicited work is that although the book may be good enough for publication, and is a viable proposition in terms of mass market sales, a similar novel may recently have been published. Or the subject matter may be out of fashion or overused. Trends within the horror genre come and go, what is in vogue today is outdated by tomorrow. Many of these trends are hard to understand. Why is it that vampire themes enjoy more popularity than werewolf ones as a general rule? The occult was in favour a short time ago, then suddenly no publisher wanted books with that theme. Then psychological horror became popular; now there is such a glut of these books, covering many variations, that perhaps they, too, have had their day. There seems no logic to market trends except that it is often governed by the latest blockbuster movie - for a short time.

I deliberately did not advise the prospective writer to study the bookstalls prior to searching for an idea, expanding it and compiling a synopsis, because by the time he or she had reached the completed manuscript stage then the entire horror publishing scene might have changed yet again. Far better to look at current trends when you have a book ready for submission. That way you might just be in time for the latest swing to whatever. Or you might catch the next trend in its infancy, which is no bad thing.

There is no short cut to finding a publisher willing to accept your book but there are ways of reducing those colossal odds against rejection after rejection.

Vanity publishers

This is virtually a guaranteed way of getting your book into print - provided you have got plenty of money to invest in it with very little chance of seeing any return for your investment in the way of sales or royalties. In effect, you are paying to have your book published.

I know one or two people who have found their way into print this way. There are a number of these publishers who advertise widely and they do not appear to have any difficulty in finding customers. Only a few weeks ago, at the time of writing, I received a phone call from somebody asking my advice. He had written a 60,000-word novel and submitted it to a vanity publisher. They had accepted it, his excitement was only tempered by the overall fee they were asking - £6,000. Yes, they would even undertake some editing that was necessary, print and bind the book and list it in their catalogue, but he was expected to buy a minimum of 500 copies to sell himself. At a 'tempting' 35% discount that would add around another £5,000 to the original quotation. 35% is the standard trade discount for booksellers, sometimes even higher, so vanity publishers are not really giving a huge concession. In a lot of cases they are using the author as both distributor and bookseller at a considerable saving to themselves.

Self-publishing

If you are willing to pay to have your book published, then the cheapest way is to shop around printers for prices and you would probably see your book printed and bound for less than half that which my acquaintance was quoted. But you will have to sell the copies yourself - if you can find a distributor to take you on, they will ask 33 ⅓% of the cover price and they will not guarantee sales; there will be a lot of 'returns' because you are a new author with no proven track record and no publicity - unless you are prepared to invest heavily in that, too. And, of course, you would need the best cover for the book you can get and artists are not cheap. We shall look at how important covers are to book sales in the next chapter.

So, my advice is the same as I gave to my caller the other week -

forget it! I have one absolutely inflexible golden rule - never pay for publishing. You don't pay to write, you write to earn money!

Literary agents

Literary agents do not guarantee an easy way into publishing. Often it is as difficult to persuade an agent to take you on their list of authors as it is to sell your work directly to a publisher. Some publishers state on their rejection slips that they are not prepared to consider manuscripts other than those submitted through a literary agency. As agents are inundated with manuscripts from new authors, the door is firmly closed to the first-time writer. Which, in my opinion, is unfair. Agents often give preference to established writers with a good track record because their books are that much easier to sell.

I have been with agents in the past. As in every other profession, there are good, mediocre and bad agents.

Don't waste time and postage by sending your manuscript unsolicited to an agent. The odds are that it will lie there until you write to enquire its fate and then, eventually, it will be returned with a compliments slip advising you that they are not accepting any new clients.

If you decide to try agents, phone first. If you receive a positive response they will ask to see your work. A month is a reasonable time for either agents or publishers to look at your manuscript and make a decision. Don't be lulled into thinking that 'no news is good news'. It generally isn't, they haven't got round to reading your manuscript and unless you remind them, they won't. New work is the first to be pushed to one side in busy times; the fact that it represents months of toil on your behalf is of no consequence to them.

I once had a manuscript gather dust with an agency for several years. Although they were handling three or four horror titles a year for me, they were not keen on the fact that I had written a children's book. Eventually, I left that agency and sold the book myself; it led to a regular series with a major publisher.

Agents are advantageous to a new writer in so much that manuscripts submitted to a publisher by an agent will usually be looked at more speedily than those offered direct by the author. Agents will not offer unpublishable work so an editor is more likely to give consideration to something that has already been 'vetted'. Agents do not have any influence on publishers' decisions but in the case of a new writer extra attention will be given to the work. Agencies exist on the strength of the commissions they earn so they will do their utmost to sell your work.

An agent's commission charge is usually 10% of all monies received by them on the book; this includes an advance, royalties, translation rights etc. The publisher's contract will be with the author but the money will be paid over to the agency who will deduct their share and send you the balance.

An agent's job is to sell your work and to negotiate the best possible terms for you. The agent will discuss these matters with your publisher but the contents of the book, apart from the agent's initial judgment which will determine whether or not he accepts you as a client, are strictly between you and your editor.

Never rewrite or revise on an agent's advice. It might even be a ploy to keep you busy when he has failed to sell your book! Who knows? Agents are not authors. If they were then they would concentrate all their efforts on selling their own books. Take heed of their advice, certainly, for many have had years of experience in publishing, but remember, you are the boss, the agent is your employee and his wages have to be earned by placing your work with a publisher.

Basically, the agent's 10% fee buys experience and a contract. An agent knows which publishers are buying what books and he also knows the editors of those publishers. Consequently, his task is that much easier than yours, he has a head start where contacts are concerned, but that is no guarantee that he will sell your work. It merely improves the odds.

He should be an expert where contracts are concerned, and it is in his interest to obtain the best possible deal for you. Contracts are something which we shall look at shortly (see page 65).

I had had several books published before I employed an agent. I thought at the time that I might improve my deals if an agent was representing me. It did not work out that way; I was well known to all the paperback houses and they were not prepared to make any major changes in my contracts just because an agent was working on my behalf. In effect, I sold more of the same kind of horror novels for much the same money as I was getting before; one or two slight improvements in my contracts were successfully negotiated but nothing that warranted the 10% that was deducted from every cheque I received. In effect, I was paying somebody to do something which I had been doing myself for a number of years previously.

So I reverted to handling all my own deals again.

Beware, an agent can lose you a deal. Sometimes when a manuscript has been going the rounds of publishers and you have virtually given up hope, an editor somewhere will come up with a small offer out of the blue. Understandably, you are excited but your euphoria may be dashed because your agent states categorically that the deal isn't worth it and he is sure he can find a better offer elsewhere. My advice is, take any offer when the chips are down. The ultimate decision is yours; an agent has no right to turn anything down without consulting you first.

Many years ago a well-known agent told me that my work was too good for mass-market horror. She advised me to write a couple of 'novels', uncommissioned and without any pressure, and to take my time over them. I was new to agents then and I took her advice; I spent a whole year without any advances and handed over the manuscripts to the agent. She told me a month later that if she couldn't sell these then she would travel up to my home and eat her hat in front of me. I'm still waiting for her to arrive!

Those particular manuscripts I revamped into horror books and sold them at the first attempt! Talk is cheap, action is costly; fortunately, I recovered my outlay of labour on those books but I might well not have done.

But as a new writer you will be gambling your work on the open market and presumably you have some sort of income so you will have to be patient. Agents can be a bonus to an unknown writer and, likewise, household names need agents to push for an extra million on their advances. The bread-and-butter writer does not need an agent, he can't afford one; he knows where to offer his work, the kind of money to expect and he has a fair knowledge of contracts. Why should he pay somebody 10% just to do the paperwork?

By all means try to persuade an agent to take you on his books, you have nothing whatever to lose at this stage. But if you have not sold your novel in a year or so, then sever all connections with that agency and try the market yourself. At least you will not do any worse!

Or perhaps you would prefer to try to place your work with a publisher yourself. It can be an exciting game and your chances are infinitely greater than winning the lottery or the football pools. There will be disappointment when you find that familiar self-addressed package in the porch but there is always next time. You have to be optimistic; great writers have played this game for a long time before eventually they found success; books, which subsequently earned fame and fortune for their authors, have had a string of rejections before some far-seeing editor has put his reputation on the line and bought them.

Whether you try for an agent or 'go it alone' is up to you. It is a personal choice, I can only advise on the pros and cons of both.

Submitting your work

Again, a reminder about the presentation of manuscripts. Mine have, until recently, had a rubber band round them to keep the pages together and have then been slipped into a polythene freezer bag. The idea is to keep your typescript as tidy as possible because if your luck isn't in, and the book is frequently going back and forth, those pages soon become dog-eared.

That is the theory, anyway! In practice, that same neat package comes back to me in due course and I can see at a glance that the contents have not even been taken out of the bag. An accompanying printed slip reads 'having carefully read your manuscript, we regret that we are unable to accept it for publication....'

Or . . . the manuscript is returned, a jumble of creased loose A4 pages, without the original rubber band to hold them in place, just shoved in a jiffy bag. Now, even after time spent sorting and trying to smooth out the creases, the book takes on a 'well-submitted' appearance. So I now put the manuscript in a rexine folder, the pages bound so that they cannot come loose. Do NOT use a ring-binder; the punched holes in the pages tear and after a couple of submissions editors won't bother to read it; it has most certainly been rejected before, and what wasn't good enough for the previous editor will not be for the current one. A little deception is a distinct advantage, give your offering the look of a first-time submission.

First, though, you have to determine which publisher is most likely to buy the type of book you have written.

Writers' and Artists' Yearbook is published and updated by A & C Black annually. It is an excellent guide to just who is publishing what. You really do need the latest edition, though, because in this day and age publishers fold, are taken over, merge and new firms spring up which will not be listed in last year's edition. An up-to-date copy is invaluable, you will refer to it again and again. However, you will need more than a reference book if you are going to target the publishers who cater for horror. Guides can not give you precise up-to-date details of which area of a genre publishers are specializing in now.

Genres go in and out of fashion and, at the time of writing, horror fiction is not top of the mass market league. Don't get dejected, though, because original horror is still being published and, as his-

tory has proved, it will make a comeback. Two years from now publishers could be crying out for horror and now is the time to get
your foot in the door, edge it open and creep inside, become established for when a boom recurs. You must continue to think posi-
tively; you must have a positive attitude otherwise you would not
have embarked upon the mountain of work which has enabled you
to have a horror novel packed up and ready to send off. You must
now set about a different kind of research.

Now is the time to make some lengthy visits to bookshops.
Armed with a notepad, study the shelves and see who is publishing horror and by which authors. And, most important, see what
kind of horror they are publishing; it is no good sending a pulp-
type novel to a publisher who specializes in sophisticated psychological horror. Check also to see if books are UK editions of USA
publications; some publishers rely almost exclusively on the
American market; it is often much cheaper to buy the rights of an
American book than to purchase home-grown material, and if the
book has done well in the States, it stands a good chance of becoming successful in the UK, too. It lessens the publisher's risk factor,
which is no consolation to the aspiring British writer. Look for publishers of original horror fiction; you will be wasting your time submitting to those who specialize in reprints.

It is also worth checking on the publication dates of any horror
novels whose publishers might suit you. It could well be that a particular title has been published for a couple of years, by which time
the subject matter may be out of fashion. A recent reprint is a good
sign.

Hardcover or paperback?

Many paperback publishers give preference to buying the rights of
hardcover novels; sometimes there is a standing arrangement
between hardcover and paperback houses so, again, you will be
wasting your time sending your manuscript to those particular
paperback publishers.

You may decide to try a hardcover publisher first. A basic guide
to whether or not your novel is suitable for hardback is the content;
hardcover novels need to be of a high standard and must not be
laced with bad language and violence, something we have already
discussed at greater length (see page 47).

You will not receive anything approaching a paperback advance
for a hardcover book but it is an excellent springboard into paperback publishing. Hardcovers often receive reviews, paperbacks

rarely do. If you are published in hardcover, you have a head start. It does not necessarily follow that the paperback rights will be bought but there is a good chance they will.

Occasionally a publisher has suggested that a manuscript is more suitable as a hardcover. Apart from the few guidelines I have given about hardcovers you can never really know for certain. You could try a publisher who publishes both hard and soft covers.

So now you have a list of prospective publishers compiled from bookshop shelves. Compare your own list with *Writers' and Artists' Yearbook*. You will note in the latter that in most entries the names of editors are quoted. When contacting a publisher, either by telephone or letter, it is important to have a name.

Do not send an unsolicited complete manuscript. We shall deal with this aspect very shortly, but there are two ways in which to make contact with the publisher of your choice:

1) Write a short letter to the editor, enclosing a brief synopsis of your book, and enquire if the publisher would be interested in seeing your manuscript. Keep your letter short and to the point, and don't enthuse about your own work or they certainly will not want to see it.

If you have not received a reply within two weeks it is unlikely that they are interested. They are not interested in your book and they are either too rude or too lazy to reply. There is no reason why you should not approach two or three publishers at a time; it is most unlikely that more than one will express a wish to see your manuscript and you will have saved time waiting for negative or non-replies. On the rare chance that two publishers ask to see it, you can always keep one waiting.

I personally never send out more than one copy of a manuscript at a time. However, there is no reason why you should not; in the event of two acceptances, you will have to take the best offer and be diplomatic with the other. I prefer to deal with one at a time. It is a personal choice.

2) Telephone your chosen publisher. *Writers' and Artists' Yearbook* quotes telephone numbers (these are rarely given in a published novel). Ask to speak to the editorial department. As with a letter, be brief. And make sure you obtain the name of whoever you speak to or the editor to whom the manuscript will be addressed. You can often tell from their tone of voice whether or not he or she is really interested in reading your work.

Contact with a publisher has now been made. Always include return postage with your manuscript; it is only courtesy, and it may mean the difference to your work being read and, if it is rejected, you want it returned promptly. More often than not publishers ask to see a synopsis and a couple of sample chapters; manuscripts are costly to mail and the editor will have a good idea from those spec-imen chapters whether or not the remainder of the novel will be of interest.

Never give the impression that you are certain that your book will be accepted but, on the other hand, submit it with confidence. Now the nail-biting wait begins!

'The slush pile'

'The slush pile' is the name given by publishers to their ever-increasing mountain of unsolicited manuscripts. Usually these are stacked in a separate room and when the pile becomes embarrass-ingly large an editor is assigned to look at them; or they may employ a freelance reader. Whatever publishers do, generally not a lot of time will be spent on the task.

I met a 'slush pile' reader once; he claimed that he could get through a hundred manuscripts in an afternoon. His method was to open a typescript and read a page or two in the middle. If the writ-ing was of a reasonable standard, he would check the final pages to see if the quality had been sustained. If it had been then he would read some more of it. Only on rare occasions did he take a manu-script home to read in its entirety.

The authors of all these unsolicited manuscripts have not both-ered to write or telephone first, or, in some cases, to ascertain whether or not the content is applicable to the genres which the publisher publishes. Many do not include return postage; these are returned last of all.

The chances of a book being bought out of the 'slush pile' are slim. It does happen, though, but you must make every effort to prevent your manuscript from ending up here. Writing to an editor by name is perhaps the best way of ensuring that your work is looked at before some bored and unenthusiastic freelance reader yawns his or her way through the pile on that groaning desk.

Rejections

Just briefly at this stage I want you to think negatively. It will not make one jot of difference to the fate of your book but, if you assume that it will be rejected, then you will not be too disappoint-ed when it arrives back on your doorstep. This is merely conditioning yourself to reality; you will, in all probability, have to go through a number of publishers before you hit the right one.

A rejection does not mean that your book isn't any good. There are many reasons why good books are turned down. The following are just a few of the legitimate reasons for a manuscript being rejected:

- a work of a similar nature has just been published,

- publishers are constantly reducing their lists, publishing fewer and fewer titles,

- the schedule for the next two years is already filled,

- manuscripts are only considered when submitted via a literary agent (which we have already dealt with).

Occasionally one receives a personal letter stating a reason(s) why one's particular book has not been accepted for publication. Do NOT begin rewriting or revising on the strength of this; editors' opinions differ from publisher to publisher and are, in any case, just an individual opinion.

Once I was introduced to a young editor who was responsible for building up a new imprint for a major publisher. He said that he would be very interested in looking at some of my work. At that time I had had 100 books published. The following week I sent him a completed manuscript.

It was returned within a week. The reason for the rejection was, so his accompanying letter informed me, '. . . we are looking for either new writers or established authors who are well known to the book trade. As you do not fall into either category, we are unable to publish you.'

I don't know whether it was naivety or if he was being deliberately offensive. I rather think that, face-to-face, he did not have the courage to tell me that he was not interested in my work. I did not fail to notice that the typescript which I had submitted was returned unread!

There are discreet methods whereby it is possible to tell whether your work has been read. Very lightly put a small dab of glue between pages here and there, not enough to stick them firmly, just sufficient so that when the pages are turned they come apart. PrittStick is ideal for this purpose. If those pages are still adhered when you receive your book back, you will know that it has not been read.

If a typescript is returned as neatly as it was submitted, the chances are that it has not been read. When it is returned with pages upside down and back to front that is no guarantee that it has been looked at, either. The editor may well have dropped the book on the floor!

Go through a returned typescript carefully. Ideally, you want to submit it to each publisher as though it was a first offering. I have already mentioned putting it in a binder. Alternatively, it is a good idea to photocopy it after several rejections or print out a new copy if you have it on disc.

Never give up! There are times when you will feel like it, but don't. However, if those rejections persist then you might do worse than to reread your work. You may see ways in which the book can be improved.

Do not sit back and await the fate of your first book; just because it has not made publication yet there is no reason why you should not begin work on a second. As I have already said, each book should be better than your last, so your next attempt will have the benefit of your already having written a full-length book. You are gaining in experience all the time. And there is an added incentive here - if you should manage to sell your second book then the chances of your publisher buying your first are greatly enhanced.

At this stage, though, do not let any publisher to whom you submit Book 2 know that you have written another one. Wait a while and then submit Book 1 as though you have just finished it. Unless, of course, your latest work is a sequel to your first effort!

I have sold an 'oldie' on more than one occasion!

Publishing in America

There is massive potential for the aspiring writer in the USA but it is a far more difficult market to break into. In many ways British writers are at a disadvantage; the American readership is totally different, they are looking for books that are big in size and plot, ie the 'blockbuster'.

I have devoted a separate chapter in this book to American horror; see page 96. Whilst much of the advice on finding a publisher applies to the USA as well as the UK, I decided that it was preferable to deal with the transatlantic set-up separately rather than confuse the beginner with those aspects which are applicable to one but not to the other.

However, some advice on submitting material to USA publishing houses is not amiss whilst we are in the midst of dealing with that subject.

Writers' and Artists' Yearbook is again a useful guide but it is, in this case, only a basic one where the cataloguing of USA publishers is concerned. It would be a mammoth, near impossible, task to list every American publisher and their requirements. *Literary Market Place* (published by R. R. Bowker in the USA) is the most comrehensive guide to American publishers, listing what they publish. A copy from Bowker Saur in the UK will cost around £135. However, you should find a copy in a good public library. Go armed with notebook and pencil and extract the most likely looking sources for your work from its pages.

You will see from the entries in the directory who publishes what. But whatever you do, do NOT rush off a copy of your completed manuscript to some publisher in the States who you think fits the bill. The chances are that you will never see it again and you won't even get a reply. UK publishers are inundated with unwanted unsolicited manuscripts; in the States you can multiply that by 100! In my experience USA publishers are notorious for not replying to correspondence, anyway.

There is only one method of approach which is likely to bring any success at all; compile a short outline of your book and make several photocopies. Also photocopy the first chapter. At this stage multiple submissions are necessary if you are to stand a chance of receiving any replies. Enclose a copy of your synopsis, together with the chapter and a short letter. And in order to enhance your chances of a response, include some International Reply Coupons to an approximate equivalent of the outgoing postage.

Should you hear from a publisher, then you will have to send a copy of the completed manuscript. This is an expensive procedure; the postage, and it must go by airmail as a positive interest has been shown in your book, will cost you around £15 for an average typescript. In this instance there is no need to include return postage as the editor has asked to see your work and therefore should return it at his expense.

It will be a long time before you hear anything. Wait at least two months. If you have not heard by then, make a phone call. USA publishing moves very slowly. I once made contact with a publisher on the above lines and a genuine interest was shown in my proposal. An outline and specimen chapters was requested. Four months later, not having heard from the editor, I telephoned. He asked me to give him another month and assured me that everything was fine and he liked my proposal. Two months later he wrote and asked to see the rest of the manuscript. Almost a year to the day after my first approach, a deal was agreed.

American literary agents will not usually take on an unpublished British author. However, if by any chance you know somebody in the States who has some knowledge of the American publishing industry, then perhaps you can persuade him to represent you. I do this nowadays but it is necessary to know the person well and not to rely upon some 'pen-pal'. The saving in postages is enormous and the cost of phone calls are reduced considerably. We usually have an 'up-date' telephone call about once a month. He is guided by my suggestions and it works well. It also speeds up submissions and rejections.

But we will look at publishing in America in more detail in Chapter 12. If you are successful in placing your work with a British publisher then there is every chance that the USA rights will be bought and this will launch you on the American scene.

In most cases UK publishers will insist on buying world rights to your book. This means that they will attempt to sell it in the States so you can leave it in the hands of their foreign rights department. But do chase them up from time to time; telephone them to enquire if there has been any overseas interest in your book. If they attend foreign book fairs, for example Frankfurt and the ABA, then you can expect your book to be shown to overseas publishers. A foreign sale is a bonus - you don't have to do any additional work!

7

Published

Suddenly, right out of the blue, your dream has become reality! It is a moment that every writer remembers for the rest of his or her life; secretly, you never really believe that it will happen, you cling to the same hope that gives lottery and football pools punters a buzz, you are doing something that might just change your whole life. It is the dream that has kept you going throughout a humdrum routine of everyday work.

A letter arrives one morning, you see by the franking that it is from the last publisher to whom you submitted your manuscript. In all probability it is just an acknowledgment of safe receipt. Or, more likely, as has happened before, a letter informing you that 'we regret that this book isn't for us and your typescript is being returned under separate cover'.

Your fingers shake a little as you rip open the flap, any correspondence from publishers is nerve racking. You stare in disbelief at the typewritten letter, unable to take in those words '. . . we have now read your book and we would like to make you an offer . . .'

Your fingers shake uncontrollably as you read it over and over again. Perhaps you are dreaming and you will wake up any second. Or it is a mistake, you have received a letter intended for another author. Or some cruel hoax. No, it is none of these, you are now to become a published author.

You will probably go out and celebrate and I don't blame you for that. But soon you will have to come down to earth and if you don't have an agent then you will need to speak to your publisher and agree a deal.

Contracts

As a first time writer you will be offered a basic contract and you will not be in a position to negotiate very much, if at all. The publishers know that you will accept their offer because you are now one of the very few new writers who has actually managed to nudge the door open.

Gone are the days of sizable advances, except in the case of well-known writers and celebrities who often employ a ghost writer to write their books. They will be offered tens of thousands, even millions of pounds, but you will be offered a very modest sum against anything from 6% to 7½% of cover price royalties for an original paperback; the advance on a hardcover will be even lower but you should look for a 10% of cover price royalty. Small publishers might offer less. My advice is to accept whatever you are offered, at least you will see your work published and, if it sells reasonably well, you will earn royalties on top of your advance. Also, you may well sell that publisher another book in due course.

Royalties are calculated on either the sale price (cover price) of the book or on the price received for the book by the publisher. There could be a considerable difference between the two. Check your contract very carefully before signing so that you know what to expect. In most cases the royalties will be paid on a percentage of the book's cover price but in some instances, such as bulk sales to Book Clubs, your royalties will be calculated on the price received.

Until 1995 the net book agreement forbade booksellers selling a book below the cover price. Now that agreement has been broken and major bookstores are selling selected titles (usually bestsellers) at very considerable discounts. The author will receive a percentage of that sale price. In theory, more books should be sold at a lesser price but it remains to be seen whether increased sales at those discounts will financially benefit the author.

Read your contract very carefully. Reputable publishers have a standard form of contract but you must ensure that you understand it for your own protection. It is important that, having had your book accepted, you strike up a relationship with your editor. You will be working together, at least for this book, and now it becomes teamwork. You need to put a face to a name, and so does your editor. Telephone him or her; in all probability an invitation to lunch or to pop into the office will ensue. That will give you an opportunity to raise any queries which you might have about your contract.

However, it is best that you have a reasonable knowledge of contracts before that first meeting.

Option clauses

Before, you launch into writing another book, thinking that you can submit this to other publishers, it is essential that you are aware of the option clause in your contract. Virtually every publisher will insist upon one; the last thing they want is a similar book being published by a rival. And, of course, there is always the possibility that you may go on to become a bestselling author and they will want to publish you exclusively if that should happen.

The option clause, in its broadest terms, means that your publisher will have first refusal of your next work 'of a similar nature'. This means, in this case, that anything which may be vaguely classified as horror, they must consider before you offer it to another publisher. If, however, you decide that you want to attempt a book in another genre, say crime fiction or science fiction (sf), let them see your book before you offer it elsewhere. As has already been stated, the borderline between horror and sf/fantasy/crime is a very narrow one and they often overlap. Likewise, a serial killer novel may well be termed horror. Play safe, if they reject your follow-up book then you are free to try it with another publisher. But you will do well to remain with the publisher who has shown faith in you by investing in your first book until you have reason to change.

In the case of a completed manuscript being accepted for publication, your advance will usually be paid in two halves; half on signature of the contract and half on publication of your book. However, where a book is commissioned (which we will look at in Chapter 8), advances are normally paid in three instalments, a third each on signature, delivery and publication.

Contracts usually run to three or four pages in the UK; USA contracts can consist of anything up to twenty pages!

Proofs

Once you have signed your contract and received a cheque for the first part of your advance, you will not hear much from your publishers for some time. Everything is on course, they will not thank you for repeatedly writing or telephoning 'just to check'. The wait for publication date will seem interminable but you must be patient. In this instance, assume that 'no news is good news'.

At some stage you will receive a questionnaire from the publicity department. This is standard procedure with most publishers as they list all forthcoming titles in a catalogue and include brief biographical details of the author. Don't get excited and think that they are going to launch into national newspaper and London Underground advertising! They have an advertising budget and, as a new writer, you will be allocated only a minimal share of this, if any at all.

About six months prior to publication date you will receive a set of proofs for correcting. The editors usually want these completed and returned within a week or so. There are probably four or five sets being read in addition to those sent to you and, when these are completed by the various readers, the amendments will be collated on a master copy which will then be returned to the typesetter for the final printing.

Do take extreme care in checking proofs. Consult your *Writers' and Artists' Yearbook* where you will find a section on proof reading and the symbols which are to be used for corrections. Publishers and typesetters use these symbols in the same way that a reporter uses shorthand and they will appreciate your using them, too.

The correction of proofs must be given priority. The standard of typesetting varies; I have known as few as a dozen errors in 250 pages; once I had a bad set with mistakes on every page. I like to read proofs in sessions of about an hour, then take a break. Concentration lapses if you read for too long at one sitting.

Return your corrected set of proofs as soon as possible.

Covers

I cannot stress too strongly the importance of a good cover on a book. Chain bookshops will sometimes take a title on the strength of the cover alone; likewise, a casual buyer in the bookshop will often be tempted by the cover and the 'blurb'.

Unfortunately, you are unlikely to have any say contractually in the cover of your book but you can express an opinion. It is in your publisher's interest to see that your book is given the right cover.

Horror covers have changed drastically in style over the last decade. During the pulp era, and the 'mushroom' publishing of the 1950s and 1960s, there was some superb artwork but, sadly, it would not sell books today. Lurid covers have been replaced by sophisticated ones; a subtle representation of the horror portrayed within the pages is far more effective than some outlandish creation of monsters or pure gore.

You should receive a cover proof of your book. If you have not had one a month or so before publication, request one. It will give you a good idea of how your book will look on the shelves.

Cover 'blurb' is almost always written by somebody in the editorial department. It is a designated job and even if you submit your own blurb it almost certainly will not be used. The blurb is an integral part of the cover, a précis of the story but written in such a way that it is an advertisment for the book.

Publication date

Be sure to find out exactly when your book is going to be published. Sometimes publishers' schedules are changed and yours could be one of the titles deferred until a later date. If you have established a relationship with your editor at the outset then there is every chance that you will be advised of any changes.

If you have not received copies of your book about three weeks before the publication date, contact your editor to make sure that everything is on target. You will need to know when your book will be in the shops in order to do whatever you can to publicise it, something which we shall look at in the following chapter. If you have already contacted your local newspaper, and they plan to do a feature on you, then you will look rather silly if you have to tell them the week before that the book has been delayed.

Author's copies

Depending upon the terms of your contract, you should receive between six and twelve free copies of your book shortly before publication. You will have the option to purchase more at a discount if you so wish.

It is always tempting to give copies to friends but don't be too generous, apart from immediate family. I remember when my first book, *Werewolf by Moonlight* was published I gave away most of my freebies. The book sold about 15,000 copies and was not reprinted. Nowadays copies in good condition command £50 on the collectable market. I just wish that I had bought an extra couple of dozen.

It is worth noting at this stage that somewhere in your contract it will state that if the title is to be remaindered then you will be able to buy copies at the designated remainder price. In several instances over the years I have not been informed of remaindering plans and the first I have known about it has been when I saw copies in discount bookstores. Once, in my early days as a writer, the rights on a title were reverted to me and then the publishers reprinted and continued to do so for several years afterwards. This was an oversight rather than deliberate intent; I had filed their letter and forgotten all about it until I chanced to come across it some five years later. However, I did benefit from all those royalties, the book's sales picked up rather than sinking without trace into obscurity.

Keep a check on remainder bookshops in case your book should show up there. If it does, check to see if it is in any way damaged;

often copies are stamped 'damaged' when there nothing visibly wrong with them. It could just be that a batch of your books have been distributed to this source, stamped 'damaged', as an additional source of income for the publishers out of which they do not have to pay you any royalties. Few reputable publishers, if any, will stoop to this but you should keep an eye on this end of the market.

Anyway, so far, so good. You have achieved your ambition to become a published author. The most difficult hurdle of all has been surmounted but you don't want to be just a one-book author. You now need to consider your future very carefully.

Whilst you must be co-operating with your publishers in every way in order to make your book a success, you must think about a second book, maybe compile a few ideas at this stage. Whatever you do, don't abandon writing; keep your hand in. You may care to try a few short stories (see Chapter 9). It would be a mistake to rush straight into the actual writing of a second book without careful thought and planning. Plan it, think about it, decide whether or not you are going to continue in the same field of horror fiction.

You still have a part to play in promoting your book; you must, at least, be seen to be doing something. Just as in wage-earning employment, willingness and enthusiasm count for much. Your editor will appreciate your co-operation in attempting to bring your book to the notice of the public. Your efforts will be rewarded in the future.

8

After publication

I will never forget the day when I saw my first book on the shelves of a major bookshop. It took some diligent searching to locate it; there were just three copies, insignificant amidst twenty or so other horror titles, posters and dump bins for those already famous in the genre predominated. It didn't matter that mine was not some massive tome, prominently displayed in the bestseller section, it was just the fact of being there amongst the others that counted. You will experience that feeling, I assure you, when your first book is in print. No matter how many other books you write, or if you never produce another, nothing can take those few euphoric moments away from you.

The temptation is to introduce yourself to the manager of the shop, or announce to one of the sales assistants who you are. Don't. It is extremely unlikely that they will have heard of either you or your book. Booksellers concentrate on displaying big names and bestselling titles, for them the rest are also-rans. I heard recently that 80% of the horror sales of one of the largest multiple bookstores are derived from about three leading authors in the genre. Everybody else accounts for the other 20%. This may well be true, we live in an age of hype. Publishers make huge investments in those few writers, the others have to be content with the crumbs - or take steps to publicise themselves. In any case, you cannot reasonably expect to start at the top, you must work your way up, not sit back and hope that publishers and booksellers will give you a leg up. They will not. At this stage they are not interested in you other than as a shelf-filler.

Do not call your publisher to ask what the pre-publication orders (subscription figures) are. The response will be a sigh, a pause, and then you will be told that at this stage no figures are available. That may, or may not, be true in this computerized age. The fact is that publishers are unwilling to give subscription figures to a new author. There will inevitably be returns; if bookshops have not sold out your book within a certain time, copies will be removed from the shelves, the front covers torn off and returned to the distributor. The books themselves will be pulped. What a waste, I can hear you saying, and I agree wholeheartedly. Your royalty account will be debited with those unsold books. So, understandably, publishers are unwilling to release initial sales figures which may raise your hopes only to have them dashed at the end of the royalty period.

The old adage that patience is a virtue is never more true than in the case of a first-time author. In the meantime, though, there is much that you can be doing to promote sales and to reduce your 'returns'.

Publicity

As your publisher is unlikely to promote your book other than to send out press releases and list it in a catalogue, you must do everything within your power to get yourself and your book known.

Contact your local and regional newspapers, they will most certainly be interested. They are usually on the lookout for material and writers are not exactly in abundance. I have, for many years, set books in a specific locality and that aids publicity. It invariably sells books locally; people like to read about places they know or live in, regardless of the genre.

Ring up a local radio station, they are always looking for people to interview. My own experience, though, is that newspaper coverage sells more books than talking about your work on radio. This is because the local newspaper is there to be read at leisure; a radio programme comes and goes, there is no second chance to listen to it. That which interests somebody at the time is soon forgotten amidst the bustle of daily routine. But, at least, local radio will get YOU known.

Make sure that all the bookshops in your area know about your book. They may or may not order copies. Unfortunately, in the case of corner shops that sell just a few books, they leave their choice of stock to their supplier. But it is well worth a try, if they only order one copy, customers will see it and it may lead to repeat orders.

It is a good idea to type up your own Press Release and photocopy it. This saves much letter writing or lengthy explanations which are immediately forgotten. Send them to newspapers, local radio stations, bookshops and any other address where you think somebody might be interested, such as the local tourist office if your setting is local. Just give information, at the moment you do not have a track record to do a self-hype. Your own opinion is the last that anybody wants to hear!

Make it known to your publisher that you are willing to do sign-ing sessions. Signings are unlikely with a first book but if a local bookshop is willing to stage one for you, don't turn the offer down. And don't expect a queue out into the street!

Rarely are signing sessions a big success except with celebrities. If a star of television is signing books, then there will be a rush to buy copies, not for the book itself but simply to meet and obtain his or her autograph.

If only a handful of people turn up, don't be disappointed. Your efforts will not have been wasted, you will undoubtedly achieve a mention in the press, however small. Glean every scrap of publici-ty that is on offer.

Horror, where some people are concerned, carries a stigma. It is not wholly acceptable as may be crime fiction and thrillers. This has, in my opinion, come about over the last four decades. In the 1950s horror comics were imported from the USA; many schools and parents banned them, and they were claimed to be a bad influ-ence on young readers. Certainly, they were graphic but they were nowhere near as violent as some of today's comics. However, the damage was done; 'horror is bad for you'. Then, more recently, came the 'nasty' videos. Some of these portrayed unnecessary gore and violence, and in many there is very little storyline. Some years ago I hired one simply to find out what all the fuss was about. Most of this particular video featured a crazed fiend on the rampage with a chainsaw. I became bored with it, the mutilations were uncon-vincing and I certainly would not have wasted a pound to watch another. Yes, video nasties are in bad taste and are most certainly not for children. Adults have a choice but, having witnessed scene after scene of bloody violence, who would then make the effort to read a book of similar content? These videos received bad press, all horror came under the same umbrella as a result. If you were known to read horror, others glanced askance at you. Thrillers are fine, but not HORROR!

However, when Stephen King became the world's bestselling author, horror began to achieve some respectability. If, as quoted, so many millions read King then there had to be some value in his books. But it set a new trend; horror must be subtle and it must have something of literary value.

You may find that there is a resistance to horror when you are asked to give interviews. A reporter once accused one of my books of being in bad taste; it turned out that he had only read one page of his review copy and taken it completely out of context! On anoth-er occasion a religious sect was calling for the Halloween festival to be banned. I was due to give a live radio interview but the station requested me to arrive in the morning, instead of the afternoon, so that the programme could be recorded and then 'vetted' by their religious expert! As it turned out, my recorded programme went on air without any cuts.

But, you have chosen to write horror; if you had not, then you would not be reading this book. So you must learn to live with unfounded criticism of the genre. Controversy is no bad thing; it may well earn you publicity that would otherwise have passed you by. After all, horror fiction is but an extension of thriller fiction that reaches those areas shunned by convention. It is a thriller novel that is both imaginative and exploratory, and is shackled neither by this world nor the next. It has no boundaries.

The fact that you have made some effort to promote your novel will, undoubtedly, have impressed your editor. But it will not be a deciding factor in whether or not the editor contracts another book with you. Nowadays, publishers are governed by their accountants and sales figures are the criteria. They have a scale of figures that represent a break-even margin. They will not tell you what those figures are but, in current times, an original paperback that sells 5,000 copies has done moderately well. Hardcovers are expected to sell around 600 of a 1,000-copy print run initially, and most of those sales will be to libraries.

In my early days my subscription figures for original horror paperbacks used to average 60,000. However, today, print runs are nothing like that, the average paperback has a printing of 7,000–8,000.

Additional income from your book

1) Foreign rights
The sale of foreign or translation rights of your book will be an added bonus. The only work you will be required to do in connection with this is to sign a contract with a foreign publisher; and if your own publisher handles the rights deals, then you won't even have to do that!

I have sold many foreign rights over the years. During 1991 I was Poland's bestselling author with a million-plus sales. I had 32 titles published within this period and I negotiated directly with the publishers myself. Foreign advances rarely match their UK or USA equivalents but, nevertheless, they are worth having. In some cases royalties are paid in advance on a specified print run. If the book goes to a reprint then the publishers have to renegotiate with a new contract. We shall cover USA rights in Chapter 12.

2) Public Lending Right

In 1984 the first PLR payments were made. They were long over-due. An author is entitled to royalties from every book he sells, so why should he not have remuneration when books are borrowed from libraries?

One of the first tasks you should undertake on publication of your book is to register it for PLR. Write and ask for a registration form from: Public Lending Right Office, Bayheath House, Prince Regent Street, Stockton-on-Tees, Cleveland TS18 1DF.

After your initial registration, all you will be required to do will be to send in a Short Application Form for each new book published or different editions of books already registered. Royalties are calculated up to the 30th June, annually. Any registrations received after that day will go into the following period.

You will have earned your PLR in the writing of your book(s) but, apart from registering each title, there is no further work needed to claim your money. Sometime in December you will receive a print-out from the PLR Office detailing your borrowings and the amounts due. The money will be paid in February.

You cannot afford to miss out on this one.

Film/television rights

Nowadays sales of film and television rights are a rarity except in the case of blockbuster bestsellers. There is no point in sending copies of your books to either movie or television companies; they simply will not be looked at. Multiply a publisher's 'slush pile' by a thousand and you might be approaching the number of submissions the visual market receives. You may not even receive a reply.

Film and television rights are a very lucky and very big bonus. Mostly they are bought through agents in the industry; I am in touch with, and have been approached by, agencies on both sides of the Atlantic. Strong interest has been shown in titles but the only film rights I ever sold came about because my book *Night of the Crabs* (1976) was a lead-title and bestseller. I guess some film producer noticed one of the bookshop displays, bought a copy and liked it. I never found out any other details. As so often happens, the film was never made,

There are many reasons why film rights are bought, even filmed, but not released. Perhaps the original backers have opted out of the deal, a distribution deal falls through, or financial problems are encountered. The reasons are manifold but if you are paid for film rights and your story makes the big screen, it is a real bonus.

Years ago I sold several film options for my books. The general rule was that companies would purchase a 2-year option for £500. It gave them time to do their costing and to see if the idea was viable without a rival stepping in and buying the rights in the meantime. I never had an option materialize but the option was good money for nothing.

Television, film and video companies are inundated with unsolicited material. Sadly, much of it never gets looked at and is returned with a polite rejection slip. Frankly, you are wasting your postage submitting your book direct to these companies. What you must target are the Production Companies, those companies who make the films and programmes for cinema, television and video. In order to obtain the addresses of these companies, you will require a copy of *Contacts* which can be obtained for a few pounds from: The Spotlight, 7 Leicester Place, London WC2H 7BP, Tel: 0171-437 7631.

What makes a bestseller?

An international bestseller is not necessarily a good book. Hype is often the key to huge sales but it needs a big name to back it up. In recent times we have seen novels under the names of famous celebrities but these have, in some cases, been written for them by ghost writers. The publishers are banking on the name selling the book rather than the story itself. Some have failed miserably and the average writer can be forgiven for showing little sympathy.

The celebrities' names alone will sell those books - in theory. Massive hypes are backed up by widely-advertised signing sessions and personal appearances. It remains to be seen if these stars will produce a follow-up book and whether or not they will succeed as writers. Initially, booksellers will stock such titles in quantity and, against a backcloth of media advertising, they are displayed prominently in all the bestseller sections.

The unfortunate part about all this is that celebrities are paid massive advances for their books and that leaves a meagre residue in the publishers' kitty to be shared out amongst those smaller authors who do not have a ready-made mantle of fame to drape over their literary efforts. A first-class novel by an unknown writer is unlikely to command a huge advance or a sizable budget to promote his book.

If the publishers have shelled out millions for a celebrity's novel, their only chance of recouping that outlay is by telling the reading public how good the book is. A novel by a lesser author has to stand on its own merits.

Consequently, booksellers are stocking the same number of books as before but by fewer authors than in previous years. They go for what they see as proven hyped bestsellers.

Apart from 'big names' there is one common denominator amongst these international bestsellers; they are virtually all huge books, 500-700 pages in length. Perhaps this is an extension of the hype; the readers think that big is 'beautiful' and that they are getting their money's worth. A writer who has purposely set out to make his or her living according to the market, and writes in commercial genres, rarely becomes a household name yet can command worthwhile sales that will ensure a good living.

Sequels

Once your first book is published and you have done your best to promote it, your thoughts will understandably turn to a second novel. We are going to consider this possibility later but it is as well to mention here the pros and cons of sequels. Your sales are good, your editor is already pleased, so have you, subconsciously, hit on a successful formula, got it just right? Who knows? You are already tempted to write a sequel to your first book. Don't! Not at this stage, anyway. Twenty years of writing experience has proved to me that sequels rarely match the original. Don't discard a sequel altogether but keep the idea for later.

Going full-time

Of course, with a reasonably successful book under your belt and a strong possibility of a second in the reasonably near future, you may be thinking of making your living out of what has previously been a hobby. You always wanted to write horror fiction, you have proved that you can do just that, so there is nothing better than giving up your boring 9-to-5 job and just writing, all day and every day.

But the prospect needs much deliberation, you must consider every conceivable advantage and disadvantage. It is not a decision to be made quickly or lightly. Your heart must not be allowed to rule your head.

Writing is a precarious occupation. Every time you write a book you never know if you will write another. Unless, of course, you are fortunate in having secured a multi-book contract. But even that, with phenomenal success, will not provide you with enough money to last you for the rest of your life.

Genres go in and out of fashion. Westerns 'died' years ago; they have never really come back. Horror fiction undergoes drastic changes as we have already seen; the animal horror stories of yesteryear were replaced with a spate of occult novels. Then the trend turned to sophisticated psychological horror. Over-saturation has been to blame in all cases. What will come next? Can you adapt to whatever becomes fashionable in order to survive?

At the height of the horror 'boom' in the early 1980s I was invited to a publisher's Halloween party. Virtually every paperback house was publishing two or three horror titles a month. I talked with several new writers at that gathering; almost every one of them had been commissioned to write a horror novel, irrespective of what they had written previously. Horror was about to become the biggest publishing phenomenon of all time, we were told.

A couple of years later that same publisher had cut the horror list drastically and retained just two authors. I was fortunate to be one of those two. But the 'golden era' had gone, sales were falling drastically. Except in a few cases, they have never recovered.

My own decision to become a full-time writer was not an instant one. At the time I had a secure job in banking and wrote in the evenings and at weekends. I had to decide whether I dare sacrifice that security for an uncertain future.

I set myself a three-year target. My aim was to pay off my mortgage and accumulate enough capital to give me a good start in my new career. In fact, I achieved my goal within two years but I stayed on at the bank for a further twelve months just to make sure that I could maintain my rate of success.

There is a vast difference between a part-time and a full-time writer apart from the loss of the security of a salary. One really must become established before taking the plunge. One or two successful books are no guarantee that an income will continue.

Ideally a full-time writer needs commissions to write books. This means that, on acceptance of a synopsis, a publisher will commission you to write the book(s). This benefits both publisher and writer; the publisher is assured of having a book which they want, when they want it. Hence, the importance of adhering rigidly to delivery dates, for the publisher will already have scheduled the work for publication. The writer will be guaranteed money up-front which will enable him/her to meet bills etc, during the writing of the book. The advance is usually paid in three equal amounts, a third on signature of the contract, a third on delivery of the manuscript and the remaining third on publication of the book. I try, where possible, to persuade a publisher to pay a large amount on signature of the contract. Money banked in advance gives one a feeling of security and, I believe, makes the writing of the book more relaxed, resulting in a better end product.

A full-time writer needs to find regular commissions; that way you are assured of a continuity of work. But, in order to achieve this security you need to have two or three reasonably successful books published first. When this happens, provided sales remain reasonably constant, publishers will prefer to commission a book from you; it helps them to organise their publishing programme in advance. It will be what they want and when they want it. They, like you, will be able to schedule accordingly.

Commissioned work creates pressure! But far better to be under pressure to deliver on time than to be struggling to sell your book.

Self-discipline is crucial now. We have already discussed its importance in the writing of a first book but now it is the difference between earning a living or being out of work. Your publishers will give you a deadline in order to allow them to schedule your next book, to tie publication in with distribution and whatever small amount of publicity they decide upon; they will need to include it in their catalogue and order form. If a writer delivers a book late then all their plans are disrupted.

Understandably, editors are not pleased when authors are late delivering a manuscript. On an isolated occasion, due to some unavoidable problem, they might be sympathetic, but perpetual lateness will not be tolerated. If you were an office worker who regularly arrived late for work in the morning, you would be sacked. Failure to meet delivery dates is no different; the publishers will have no difficulty in finding a writer to deliver on time. There are many good writers these days looking for commissions, who will work to a strict schedule.

If you meet publishers' requirements, and your books prove to be steady sellers, then, in all probability, they will be keen for you to accept a multi-book contract. Take it! You don't have to write the books, back to back, over a short period of time. Publishers will not want this, books delivered early mean that an advance has to be paid before it need be. So schedule two or three books over a reasonable period and you will be financially secure until the contract is completed.

Your aim should be to have a regular income from signature,

delivery and publication advances and, with luck, royalties as a twice-yearly bonus. Foreign rights sales will be an added benefit, if you are lucky. If you structure your outgoings within this framework, you should not have any financial problems. But always treat royalties as a bonus, never rely on them because 'returns' are an unknown factor. When you are writing books on a regular basis, by the law of averages you will always find that the sales of one are inferior to the others. You can't win 'em all!

A word of caution, everything can come to an abrupt halt for a number of reasons. Your sales might drop and if your publishers are looking for cut-backs they might decide that they can dispense with you. Editors come and go; as already stated, a good working relationship with an editor is essential but, a new editor might not like your work, for some reason, irrespective of sales. This happened to me in America a few years ago; all six *Crabs* titles were contracted. The first three were published at the same time with beautifully embossed covers. They sold reasonably well. Then came a change of editorship and the incoming editor, I was told, did not care for the *Crabs* as a series. It was a purely personal opinion but, as a result, the remaining three titles carried very ordinary, unembossed covers. Consequently, their sales did not match those of the first three so, temporarily, I was without a USA publisher.

There are many bonuses in becoming a full-time writer, though. Most important of all, you will have your freedom. Do not abuse it! Work strictly to schedule and plan your holidays to fit in with it. An unexpected fine day in the midst of a wet summer is a temptation to take the family on an impromptu trip to the coast. That's fine, provided you are on target with your work. If you are not, then despite protests, you must stay at home and catch up on your scheduled wordage.

Writing is much the same as any other job, you have to put the time in. You have to earn money. You don't work solely for money, you take a pride in your work, but at the end of the day the bills have to be paid.

Typecast?

Of course, you will be typecast if you are successful in your chosen field of writing. And I believe that that is a good thing overall. What one has to beware of is that editors tend to think that you can only write a certain type of horror. That happened to me following my success with the *Crabs* series. So I had to prove that I could write occult and psychological horror as well. In fact, I had to write an uncommissioned book to prove the point.

Pseudonyms

If you are successful, then stick with the name under which your books are published. As we have seen, it is not easy for a new writer to become published and an unfamiliar name will be treated as such by distributors, booksellers . . . and readers.

There are only really two reasons for using another name. If you are associated with a particular horror series and wish to write another kind of horror, it may be advantageous to adopt a pseudonym. There is a chance that you could damage your established name if your diversification is not a success.

When I wrote a serial killer novel, *The Hangman*, which was published in hardcover by Piatkus in 1994, I used the name 'Gavin Newman'. Certainly this book was very different from anything I had ever written before. As we know, horror and crime fiction often overlap. *The Hangman* could have been categorized as either. Also, I did not wish to deter new readers who might not have liked my previous horror.

Another reason for using a pseudonym is if you launch into a completely new field. I also write children's books under the name of 'Jonathan Guy'. If my own name was to appear on these books then, in all probability, bookshops would put them in the horror section; that would probably disappoint my horror fans and would not sell many copies to children! Likewise, parents looking to buy a book for their children for Christmas or birthdays might think that because I am a horror writer then these animal stories would be unsuitable for their offspring.

Only use a pseudonym if you are writing something different from what has gone before.

9

Short stories

We have already briefly discussed short story markets in Chapter 1. Sadly, the publishing industry seems opposed to publishing much in the way of anthologies and short stories these days but I feel that, like other genres which have 'died' and then been resurrected, the full cycle will turn and one day they will regain popularity.

Even with the current contracting market, the horror novelist should not ignore short stories. There are still several small press (amateur and semi-professional) magazines which feature short stories. As these magazines tend to come and go quickly I have not listed any, but *The Dark Side*, a horror magazine, lists fanzines which publish short stories, and the British Fantasy Society gives information on fanzines in their newsletter (see useful addresses, page 106).

Small press publications should be encouraged and supported, they are the backbone of horror 'shorts'; many of them feature contributions by well-known horror writers as well as some very good amateur fiction. The publications who pay their contributors are only able to afford a token fee, others are gratis; the stories are written for the love of the art, for short story writing is, indeed, a craft of its own.

For the novice, his or her reward is seeing the story in print and, at least, the work is in a shop window. Provided that you retain the copyright, there is nothing lost, you are entitled to use that same story again at a later date. It may well be noticed by a major publisher and the story remembered.

A short story is, in effect, a condensed novel. It has to contain all the same ingredients - a plot, strong characterization and good dialogue. In many ways it is much more difficult to write than a novel.

In my early years I only ever wrote short stories, I never even considered attempting a full-length work. My 'training' was in the children's page of a local newspaper when I was twelve years old. From there I progressed to fanzines, amateur and then professional magazines. I had 18 stories published in the legendary *London*

Mystery Magazine until its demise in 1982. Even now I am often asked to contribute to anthologies. Usually the editors of these approach established writers for contributions. The fact that some-one is preparing a collection of short stories is not generally made public, but if they have seen a story of yours in an amateur maga-zine they might just contact you.

Technique

As with a novel, you have to have an idea before you can write a story, and that idea needs to have a short, punchy plot woven round it. During the early 1970s I wrote many detective short sto-ries and learned a technique which has stood me in good stead and is also applicable to horror stories - determine the ending and then create a mystery leading up to that finale. In other words, work backwards. In this way I have produced many short stories which otherwise would have eluded me.

The ending is the most important part of all, that is what your reader will judge your story on. A 'twist' ending is ideal, provided you work it effectively. The right short sentence will end the story crisply and effectively. Whatever you do, do not try to explain the ending just in case your reader might not have grasped it. That is the equivalent of some amateur comedian attempting to explain some unfunny joke to an audience that hasn't laughed! Your job is to make sure that it is understood but at the same time it needs to be subtle. Otherwise your whole story will fall apart.

Your short story, like your book, needs a good opening para-graph, something that will make the reader want to read on. Pacing is more important in short fiction than in longer works, it is so very easy to over-write, which has a boring effect and takes the sting out of an otherwise good story. Most short stories average 3,000–5,000 words.

When an idea for a short story strikes me, I make a note of it. More often than not, the title occurs to me along with the initial idea. I usually find that if this isn't the case then a suitable title eludes me and I really have to work at it. The title is also a very important part of the concept of short story writing. Often a single word says it all. For example, 'Bewitched' might be the title of a 'possession' theme. That is far more appealing than, for instance, 'The Man Who Was Possessed'.

You will need to read some short horror fiction to 'get the feel of it'. See how various authors handle their theme, how skilled they are in producing 'twist' endings that come as a surprise. Sometimes the climax is telegraphed, you guess it after the first couple of pages. The true art of this type of fiction is to shock and surprise.

Stephen King is undoubtedly the master of the contemporary horror short story and much can be learned about technique from reading both *Night Shift* and *Skeleton Crew*. King saves the big shock for the end and delivers it with a knock-out punch. I would strongly recommend that you read *The Lawnmower Man* (filmed, as is the case with most of King's work but the written story is far better) and *Trucks*.

Virtually all H. P. Lovecraft's works were short stories. In the 'pulp era' short fiction reigned supreme along with the novella. Publishers today are adamant that there is no market for short stories but fans of the horror genre seem to think otherwise. Which is probably why the majority of horror shorts are published semi-professionally.

My own fan magazine *Graveyard Rendezvous* publishes amateur horror short stories in every issue. In fact, the Spring 1996 issue was a Fan Fiction Special. Response and sales have been very encouraging and, contrary to what publishers say, I think there is a market for this type of fiction.

When you begin writing a short story there is no reason why you should not write the end first, even if the idea is not to solve a mystery before the lead-up to it. If you can manage that then the hardest part is done. You will need to practise with a few stories in order to get the hang of the technique. Experience counts for much, as with novels.

You may, though, find the creation of characters more difficult than in full-length works, simply because your wordage is restricted and you will not have the scope to elaborate. I usually go for one particular feature or idiosyncrasy and concentrate on it. The reader's imagination will do the rest.

Types of horror

Horror themes are not so clearly categorized in short stories as they are in novels; often they do not slot into a definable type of horror. Graphic violence is unlikely to land you a sale; the idea of a 'short' is to play upon an idea and twist it out of all recognition.

I have, on occasions, begun a story supposedly written tongue-in-cheek but it has ended up as a real spine chiller. One particular story featured a monster unplucked turkey, purchased from a market stall on Christmas Eve and brought home to be plucked and dressed. The turkey wasn't dead, just stunned, and it regained consciousness in the kitchen and terrorised the unfortunate couple. The idea came from a duck left for dead on the table when I was a boy; it revived and waddled beneath the sideboard. The dog chased it and there was absolute chaos. The incident certainly repaid me years later.

Go for something quite ordinary, an everyday item, and turn it into an object of mind-blowing terror. I once used what was apparently a child's lump of modelling clay - except that it wasn't anything quite so harmless in the end; the character worked at a nuclear recycling plant and had brought home a piece of radioactive material. I called it *The Splodge*. And so on . . .

There is an element of horror in most everyday objects if you can just pinpoint it, ideas that are tailor-made for short stories but not big enough for a novel.

Agreements

When you have a story accepted for a professional publication then ensure that you have an agreement. This is a short form of contract, much the same as for a novel. Generally, in the case of a compilation of stories by different authors, a small advance is paid for each and after that royalties are shared on a pro rata basis. The editor appointed to compile the anthology is given a budget initially, and he will pay each author according to that. The publishers will have contracted him to produce the book and the responsibility for paying authors will have been delegated at the same time.

Problems do arise, however. Some years ago I had a story in an anthology that was printed in several different editions with three separate publishers, and the editor was not paying out royalties. I complained to the first publisher, who had sold volume and paperback rights of the book, but they did not want to become involved.

Read your agreement carefully and make sure that you know how long the publisher has the rights to your story. After those rights have expired you are free to sell it again. In some cases I have sold a story three or four times but I have always informed the next publisher where it has appeared previously. It is deceitful to present it as an original story.

In general, magazines do not give you any form of written agreement but it is as well to scrutinize the small print at the foot of their letter heading. Often the terms are stated there. Mainly this is because they are buying stories and features on a regular basis and the paperwork involved in issuing agreements would be immense. It is generally accepted that they are buying First British Serial

Rights which means that six months after publication you are free to sell your work elsewhere. Usually an outright payment is made for the use of your story and no royalties are payable.

I try to write half-a-dozen short stories a year, usually between books, working from my 'ideas file'. It is good publicity, and if a reader likes your story he or she may well decide to buy your book.
Never spurn an extra opportunity to be published.

Non-fiction articles

Although this book is concerned with writing horror fiction, I think a mention of non-fiction articles and features is important. If you establish yourself as a writer of horror then it is possible that at some time you will be asked to write something for a magazine concerning the genre in which you are best known.

In this case you need to be absolutely certain of your facts. If you quote the date of first publication of a well-known novel, check it out. Do not rely upon your memory.

Non-fiction gives you the opportunity to expound your own opinions. Everybody is entitled to those! Editors like controversial articles but do not be controversial just for the sake of it. Give a balanced viewpoint, try to reason your argument, and don't be dogmatic.

If you know your subject thoroughly, there should be few problems. You need to have a starting paragraph, a lead-in, a brief mention of what it all entails. Then, having examined the topic from all angles, you need a paragraph to wind it all up. A feature article that ends too abruptly leaves the reader with a sense of something that is unfinished.

Occasionally, I submit non-fiction articles to magazines on spec. Often I receive an acknowledgment from an editor, thanking me and informing me that my work will be held on file until an opportunity arises to use it. Sometimes it is never published. This is hardly fair to a professional writer; the publishers are hedging their bets. If at some time in the future they suddenly find themselves short of material then they have something in reserve. Mostly such articles are published and paid for within a year but there is always that chance that the work may never be used. It is as well to make a diary note for a few months hence and chase them up. Unused work is wasted work for there is always the possibility of selling it elsewhere. Don't let it gather dust in their files for too long. If the subject matter is topical, the feature will become dated.

10

Children's horror fiction

Children's horror stories are by no means a new concept but it is only in recent years that this type of fiction has been categorized as such. I well remember in my childhood being fascinated by the original Mary Tourtel 'Rupert' stories - these were not the colourful, cheerful annuals with which we are all familiar today but full-length black and white illustrated books featuring witches, dwarfs and ogres and the like, mostly set in dark forbidding woods with stunted oaks. I was scared when I read them but how I enjoyed them! I don't remember having any nightmares that could be directly attributed to them.

Horror was published for children in those days but we simply never thought of it as such. Nowadays it is emblazoned on eye-catching displays in bookshops; you can't miss it.

Ladybird Books set a nice trend in their familiar hardcover well-illustrated series 'Ladybird Horror Classics'. These included abridged versions of *Frankenstein*, *Dracula* and *The Strange Case of Dr Jekyll and Mr Hyde*. A good choice from the many they could have published in juvenile form, but most of all I applaud them for their version of Sir Arthur Conan Doyle's story *Lot 249*, which they retitled *The Mummy*. This is arguably the best of the 'Mummy' stories written over the last century and shows a discerning taste in horror by the editors.

Children's horror fiction gained momentum and reached a peak in the early 1990s. Clearly, this genre of children's publishing is going to be big business over the next few years so the writers of adult horror books should at least familiarize themselves with the format.

R. L. Stine is, arguably, the most widely read children's horror author. The reader is advised to read his books (published in the 'Point Horror' series by Scholastic) and learn from them. I would recommend *The Baby Sitter* which illustrates the best in teenage terror and how to write it. For younger horror fiction, read the 'Goosebumps' series (also published by Scholastic).

Hauntings rather than horror

Children's horror is ghostly rather than horrific. Tingle those young spines but don't have their hair standing on end, and if their parents are awoken in the nocturnal hours by their offsprings' nightmares then there will be a few letters of complaint on their way to the publishers.

You need to come up with an original idea, of course. Ghosts who parade around ruined battlements with their heads tucked under their arms won't see publication. Think of something more subtle, a seemingly everyday encounter between a child (check the age group you are writing for) and somebody who seems a little strange. Don't telegraph the spectre to your readers, maybe introduce a red herring. And it needs to be action all the way, youngsters become bored with slow beginnings.

Some excellent examples of this type of ghost story are to be found in *Ghost Stories* (chosen by Robert Westall and published by Kingfisher). Here we have 22 spooky stories, a rich mixture for the reader to read and think about. There are some classic authors included in this compilation: Charles Dickens, Ray Bradbury and M. R. James to mention just three.

Simple prose

Children's books vary in length according to the age group which you are writing for. There are plenty of books available in major bookshops to give you an idea of what you are aiming at; many shops have a whole section devoted to 'Young Horror'. Do as you did initially with adult horror; check publishers, content, length and decide which you are going to go for.

If you are writing for the age group 7–9, the stories have a length of only around 2,500 words. It sounds like a short story which, in fact, it is but there is a very big difference. You won't write one in a day, not satisfactorily, anyway. Certainly think in terms of a short story; you will need to invent a 'twist' ending otherwise it will seem rather pointless. But every sentence, every word, will need to be carefully considered. Your aim is simple prose but you must not underestimate your young readership. Mostly, they are intelligent, they would not be reading books outside school if they weren't. Don't 'write down' to them, that way you will be insulting them.

Obviously there are taboos; no sex or violence should be included. Political correctness has to be considered with even more care than when writing horror fiction for adults.

Illustrations are an integral part of any children's fiction. Whilst one of the greatest pleasures in reading is in using one's imagination to conjure up characters and settings, children need a little help. If the artwork is good, and it must be for the book to be successful, the young reader will envisage a character based on the artist's portrayal and that will stick in his or her mind. Also, artwork helps to break up what otherwise might appear to be page after page of 'boring' text. Each page should be a lively mixture of illustrations and text. If the pictures are appealing then the child will be encouraged to read on.

The writer must always bear in mind that the story will be illustrated. Do not go into too much descriptive detail; just enough, the artist will do the rest. Work out in your own mind what part of the text might be chosen for illustration and where it will go in the book. It is best to seek editorial guidance at the outset. Although most children's stories are short and simply written, some rewriting might be requested. This is no reflection upon the author who must accept it as a 'learning' process, a formula that needs to be perfected for the future.

Teenage horror

There is an ample market here, too. Go along to that same bookshop and take a look, it will probably overwhelm you at first glance! One of the most prolific publishers is Scholastic Publications with their series 'Point Horror', just look at the titles in print and those being sold as 'collections', such titles as *The Return of the Vampire*, *The Fever*, *Halloween Night* and many more. What, then, is the difference between teenage horror and adult horror?

Basically, those who have been weaned on children's horror will move on to more mature books as their reading age progresses. No longer are they interested in profusely illustrated books, they are able to cope with text and they are also seeking something more frightening than spooks. That does not rule out ghost stories but here they need to have a much more sinister portrayal. Vampires, it appears from the stories in print, are very popular but there seem to be ample gothic themes available. Look for something that has not already been covered. That is not easy but if you go for the obvious, and are successful in getting into print, you will only be taking a small share of that particular field. List what has already been done then try to find something that hasn't.

If you have already had an adult horror book published, then concentrate on a fairly detailed outline for teenage terror. It is worthwhile enclosing a copy of your published book when you submit your idea to a teenage horror publisher; editors are more likely to consider writers who have already proved themselves in what is not exactly a different genre. Editors will undoubtedly ask to see specimen chapters as proof that you can adapt to writing for a younger readership.

As a rough guide, teenage horror is principally aimed at readers in their early 'teens; several of my own fan club members are in the 16–19 years age bracket; they have already moved on to adult reading and are unlikely to be interested in books for younger teenagers.

Most of the rules which apply to children's horror are applicable to teenage horror; cut out the sex and graphic violence, and avoid drugs except perhaps to portray an addict as a 'baddie'. These books are not intended to be moralistic but adolescent readers are impressionable.

Characterization is even more important in children's and teenagers' books than it is in adult fiction. Young readers like to identify with their heroes, to imagine themselves experiencing the same adventures as those fictional characters. Give them a good example to follow, and seize the opportunity to create a character whose popularity might run to a series. Series are very popular in this region of the horror genre.

Teenage books will, on average, be around 40,000–50,000 words in length and it needs to be action all the way!

11

Graphic novels and comics

Graphic novels have been around for a long time. In effect, they are comic books although the modern versions are slightly more sophisticated than their predecessors. The American horror comics of the 1950s caused a parental outcry and were subsequently banned in the UK. Prior to that the USA comic books of the 1930s (*Batman, Superman, Detective Comics*) were no less than graphic novels.

My introduction to what would today come under this category were the Classics Illustrated comics which were first published in the States in 1941 and were then reprinted in British editions by Thorpe & Porter in 1951. There were about 170 titles in all and some of these included the expected horror ones, *Dracula, Frankenstein* and *Jekyll & Hyde*. They were far superior to the black and white horror comics which had been sneaked into the UK.

In those days comics were looked upon as inferior reading material but nothing could have been further from the truth. The artwork in the Classics Illustrated series was superb and copies which have survived command astronomical prices. They were educational; in many cases children who read them went on to read the original classics which they might not otherwise have done.

The 1970s saw comics (they were still called 'comics') command a large share of the reading market. The American giants (Marvel, DC etc,) began producing dozens of titles on a monthly basis, new 'Super Heroes' were born and an exciting trend was set.

Then came what are now classified as Graphic Novels, and it was horror which dominated. The format changed from that of the comics; they resembled an A4 book with semi-stiff covers, the paper was of a high quality and the style of artwork changed, modern art as opposed to those meticulously drawn strips of the 1970s. Some were in full colour throughout, the cheaper ones were black and white. They attained cult status with their own following, devotees who preferred fully illustrated stories to text.

Some publishers now concentrate almost exclusively on graphic productions. In major bookstores graphic novels have their own stands set apart from the conventional books. Clive Barker was one of the well known horror writers to launch into graphic novels and others soon followed. Publishers saw a new market potential.

Writing a graphic novel

Graphic novels are worth considering even for the new writer. They are an entirely different concept and if your original idea for a book has not yet made publication there is always the chance that it might be more suited to the illustrated format. The reader needs to familiarize himself/herself with the general layout of graphic novels. Waterstones always carry a good selection. Titan Books is one of the main publishers concentrating on this type of publication. They have published titles by Clive Barker.

Buy a graphic novel and study it very carefully. Pay particular attention to the dialogue and captions, how much or how little written words are used, the number of frames to a page. You will need to have a good idea of the format for scripting.

Naturally, you have to have an idea, expand it into a plot and create characters. But with a graphic novel there must be action throughout. Imagine how boring it would be to read page after page of characters engaged in conversation, no matter how interesting the dialogue. Mostly long dialogue which is relevant to the story is portrayed by the artist in story 'flashback' style. You need a well-thought-out plot that is designed for action. There will be no descriptive passages, these will be conveyed visually by the artist.

Possibly the most difficult part of all will be length; you cannot plan a graphic novel in wordage. Length is determined by the number of pages (most publishers keep to a strict page length), so, having roughed out a storyline, divide it up into however many pages you are targeting. Check the number of pages in those titles in the bookshop. You then have a good guide and you will know from the outset that your length is right.

Mostly pages will contain the same number of frames and it is preferable to aim at this when scripting. If the artist decides that a certain piece of dramatic action deserves a 'splash' page (a full page illustration) then he will work accordingly. His job is to break up the monotony of page after page of the same size pictures. Unless you are working closely with an artist, aim at a standard number of frames.

Write your synopsis first and then draft the script from that.

The example of scripting on page 94 is taken from my own graphic novel, *Crab Fury*.

PAGE 1: *Splash page*. Professor Davenport sits at desk in laboratory, with worried expression.

He thinks: Can they really be wiped out? Five years since they last appeared and not a single sighting since then. Too often we thought they were finished and then . . .

PAGE 2:

Frame 1: Attractive wife stands in laboratory doorway, wears nightdress, dischevelled as though she has got up from bed.

Pat Davenport: Cliff, it's long past midnight. You can't keep this up, day after day, night after night. The crabs haven't been seen for years. . . because they're dead. Finished! Can't you understand that?

Frame 2: Close up. Professor Davenport looks up, features haggard.

Cliff Davenport: They've fooled us before and they'll do it again. I know they're lying low somewhere in the oceans of the world . . . Spawning, massing for their next assault on mankind. I've fought them too many times not to heed a hunch.

And so on . . .

Your dialogue has to be concise, you must convey through speech much of what you would write at length in a novel. Short, terse dialogue adds to scenes of action and drama. The artist will do the rest.

The artist

I was fortunate when I wrote the script for *Crab Fury* in that I worked in conjunction with a professional artist, Charlie Adlard. He had worked for Marvel Comics, as well as several other major publishers of this type of material, and we were able to make life easier for each other. He knew what he could draw best and which scenes were best depicted as a full page.

In most cases publishers of graphic novels will use their own team of artists. Thus your script has to be very clearly defined. The artists are at liberty to change a panel if they wish. Their work is much more difficult than yours for every one of your scripted frames has to be interpreted and translated into a visual image.

The finished novel will probably be much different from what you envisaged. You must accept this. With films, television and videos, you provide the idea and script writers may change it for a variety of reasons, perhaps because it comes over on celluloid

This page is from the author's graphic novel *Crab Fury*, published by Black Hill Books. It demonstrates how dialogue is scripted and is also used in a flashback scene.

better in the way they present it. With a graphic novel you have completed an additional step in that you have scripted it. But your characters will be depicted as the artists envisage them, the novel will be a combination of two or more people's ideas. Unless you are a competent artist yourself, the graphic novel will not be wholly your own work. You must accept that.

You may decide that your written novel might be better as a graphic novel. Personally, I would prefer to go for a completely new idea, it is much harder to reduce 400 pages of typescript to a visual script than to start from scratch. A textual work does not always come out as you envisage it in this format; much will have to be left out and then conveyed through dialogue. It can be done, of course, and often is, but it is difficult to capture the same atmosphere.

A graphic novel is certainly more difficult than a text-only book to place with a publisher, simply because there are only a handful of publishers producing them. Currently, publishers of graphic novels include Titan, HarperCollins, Marvel, DC and Caliber. Soon your proposal will have gone the rounds, there will be nowhere left to submit it. Another means of contact is to find out where and when a comic art convention is being held and go along; they are usually well attended by fans, artists, writers and publishers. Here you will come across a display of all kinds of artwork, magazines and books. Find out who is publishing what, perhaps chat to a few editors on their stands. You may decide to try something altogether new as a result.

Go and browse in a specialist comic shop. Forbidden Planet in London stocks just about every publication available. Here you will find comics and graphic novels as well as information regarding forthcoming comic art conventions. The staff are knowledgeable and will answer your queries. They also have a mailing list of all their titles. Send an SAE to Forbidden Planet, 71 New Oxford Street, London WC1A 1DG Tel. 0171-836 4179.

Graphic novel publishing is still small but it is a steadily growing industry. The horror writer should not ignore the potential of any branch of his or her chosen genre.

12

American horror
fiction

So far we have only looked at ways and means whereby a manuscript can be submitted to publishers in the United States of America. Now we must suppose that the writer has decided to write a horror book with the American market specifically in mind. It is a daunting task for anyone living outside that country, formidable to those who have never even travelled there, for then the problems are manifold.

On the positive side there are far more horror fiction publishers in America than in any other country. *The Literary Market Place*, mentioned on page 63, lists virtually every publisher, but it will not give you an insight into the ingredients of a novel that will stand any chance of seriously being considered for publication.

American horror fiction covers every aspect of the genre, and more. Your first step should be to buy and read a varied selection of USA horror books. They are obtainable at specialist bookshops in the UK. One store that springs to mind instantly is Murder One or one of the branches of Forbidden Planet (see Useful Addresses, page 105).

When you begin reading USA horror books you will understand what I mean. The books are big and so are the plots. All right, you think you can cope with that.

Now we come to the real problems. Most American horror is set in the States, not just well-known places like New York which you see frequently on television, but in far flung towns and landscapes that have not changed much since the frontier was won.

Are you able to research such places well enough to write convincingly about them? You think you can? Fine, off you go to the library to borrow some geographical reference books, then on down to scour the travel agents to pick up as many brochures as you can on the States.

You have worked out a big plot; on rereading it sounds credible, just the kind of novel that would stand comfortably alongside those which you have read.

Now, what about characters? And sub-characters? Whatever you make them, their lifestyles will not be anything like those of anybody you know in Britain. You will need to know the make of car your hero drives, his brand of cigarettes if he smokes, what he eats and a whole lot more that is taken for granted, that you would not otherwise even notice. If he is a police officer then you will need to familiarize yourself with American police procedure, and that varies from state to state.

Ideally, the only way is to visit that part of the States where you are going to set your novel. The cost of the trip will swallow up most of the advance that you hope to get. But maybe you have not gone full-time yet and you still have a salaried job. You have promised your partner a holiday in the States for years, and this might be your last chance. Kill two birds with one stone and research your proposed book to the full.

Let us suppose that you have decided to use New York as your setting. That would be my choice and not just because I know it reasonably well. New York City has virtually everything that a novel needs and it is fairly easy to research. One tip at this stage, walk everywhere you go; I did, covered around seven miles a day, and I can remember most of the city far better than if I'd toured it by bus or taxi. On foot you notice places, people; you have time to linger over anything that is of particular interest to you.

Every waking moment, consciously or subconsciously, will be research. You need to know streets and how people drive and walk them, 'delis' and the kind of food you can eat in them, shops and what they sell (don't forget the importance of brand names), hotel and travel procedure. Pick up every free leaflet you see even if you think you will never need it. It is amazing what unfolds within the writing of a book. And don't forget your camera; shoot plenty of film, when you're back home working at your desk NYC is a long way from home!

You think you have got it all, I'll bet you haven't. There's always something that crops up as you write that stumps you, usually a triviality, but you have to get it right. A glaring faux pas will destroy the credibility of the whole book.

But there are one or two ways to get round problems that arise. For example, let us suppose that your character has travelled to an area of the city which you suddenly realize you don't know as well as you presumed you did. He's gone to meet a contact in a public park, one that you never actually visited and to alter the location would unwind much of that which has gone before. Make it an indoor meeting, a hotel room; one hotel room is much the same as another, whether in New York or London.

Now there is one factor which might make all the difference between acceptance and failure where your book is concerned. The idea, the plot, the setting are fine. But can you write convincingly about an American in New York City? You might think you can but your publisher reads USA manuscripts every day, that overall 'British feel' will leap out of the pages at him. You haven't noticed it, you can't help writing that way, but to a New Yorker there is something decidedly unconvincing about it. So your novel might be rejected for that reason alone and, in all probability, the true reason will not be given for fear of causing offence.

Do not despair, there is a sure way of getting round this problem, perhaps the hardest one of all. You could make your leading character British. There's nothing wrong with that, people emigrate from the UK to the USA all the time and when they arrive they have to find a job in order to live. You could even have a Brit join the New York City police.

Your story is seen through the eyes of a Brit so it needs that 'British feel' to give it authenticity. No editor can logically reject a book on those grounds - which would not be politically correct, anyway! And if your Brit makes the odd mistake, then I'm sure those in his new homeland will allow him a small margin of error!

Having gone to such lengths to produce a novel which will be acceptable to an American readership, there is yet another small entrance gate through which you might squeeze. You set your book in the degradation of a downtown area of 'the City'. City slums are much of a muchness around the world, all you have to research is national customs, drop a few hints that it is probably New York and not London or Hong Kong. Dropouts and druggies have an affinity with one another, you can produce a powerful horror book within these confines. Just don't take them into more affluent localities and land yourself in trouble.

I used this particular ploy with *Dead End* (published by Zebra, New York) but for a different reason. Without spoiling the story and risking the loss of a potential reader, I used 'the City' because there is nowhere (I hope!) like it in any city in the world. The usual conception of hell is that of a place of eternal fire and torment 'down there'. Just where, we are never told. Now in my novel, hell is just beyond the derelict downtown area where the road is closed off. Beyond the barriers is a wasteland where slums have been demolished. Enter and there is no return, for the living or the dead.

It might exist in a dozen large cities around the world. Readers may speculate, but I am no wiser than they are. I created a locality and set my plot and characters within it. It sold as an original paperback to a leading American publisher.

In another book the focal point was a time warp in which the characters found themselves. It begins with a holiday in a remote hunting cabin but when the family wakes up one morning everything has gone back a century and a half. The untamed west just after the fall of the Alamo was relatively easy to write about authentically. A writer cannot use a ploy such as this more than once but it certainly served its purpose in this instance.

Luck

All along, the writer needs a slice of luck, a book to have some particular appeal. You won't know what that is until it happens, it is not something you can forecast. But most of all you need Patience and Perseverance. Things move very slowly; after a visit to New York in which I first discussed an idea with my publishers the ultimate decision to contract the book took a year. Any attempt on your part to rush things will almost invariably result in a rejection. Curb your frustration and get on with something else. The outcome could be well worth it.

13

Your second horror novel

You have achieved your ultimate ambition, you have been successful in getting your first horror book into print with a publisher. And
during the long wait you have persevered with some short stories,
maybe even placed one with a magazine. You have every reason to
congratulate yourself but this is where I have to exert a steadying
influence.

The biggest mistake any first time published author can make is
to believe that the sale of his or her second book is a foregone conclusion. Nothing could be further from the truth. In fact, new pit-
falls have opened up and the follow-up novel will be infinitely
harder.

Enjoy your well-earned period of heady success but make it brief
and come back down to earth for you have only just started out on
that long road which, if you are not careful, will end in heartbreak
and failure.

I once attended the launch of a literary prize winning novel.
Afterwards I went up to congratulate the winner. It was the first
book he had ever attempted and he was, understandably, euphoric.

'My publishers want a second book from me', he told me excit-
edly. 'In fact, I've already made a start on it!'

He was under the impression that his second book had been
commissioned. Guarded interrogation on my part, for I was exceedingly curious, revealed that this next book had not actually been
contracted. In his naivety he had misinterpreted the option clause
in his contract as a commission, and I suspect that his publishers
had not enlightened him further. They were hedging their bets; the
published novel, in spite of being an award-winning book, might or
might not do well. If it was successful, then they would have an
instant follow-up; if it wasn't, they could reject the author's second
book. They stood to lose nothing.

Tragically, I saw some copies of that prize-winning novel in a
remainder bookshop less than a year later. I doubt whether the

author's second book was bought by his publishers.

The pressure on any writer, regardless of the genre, begins with his second book. He has set a standard, publishers and readers will not accept anything below this.

The author needs to adopt a positive frame of mind. What he has done once, he can do again. Only he needs to do it better than previously.

It is most unlikely that a second book will actually be commissioned, certainly not until sales figures and returns are known for the first novel, by which time Book Number Two will probably have been written, anyway. If the first book has met, or exceeded, the publishers' expectations then it is reasonable to request them to commission Book Three on publication of Book Two. But, for the moment, we will concentrate on the second book.

If your first book features a prominent character, perhaps an occult detective, then it is a good idea to use him in your follow-up book. Treat the book as a separate novel, though. Do not make it a sequel or an obvious number two of a series. Sequels have a habit of falling short of the original, and a series needs to become well established before the books are numbered in sequence. An ongoing character is a good idea, many television series have originated from just a couple of books about the same character(s).

Allow yourself plenty of time to work out the new plot. Use your accepted book as a guide and compile a 'Characters File' so that you get every little detail right on the second time around.

Sometimes it is a good idea to alter the lead character's circumstances, maybe a change of partner or a different car, that way it gives the feel of a new book and not just volume two of the original. Make some references to any changes which you decide upon, though, or your readers might think that you have slipped up!

The preparation of your second book should be much the same as your first except that this time you will work much more confidently in the knowledge that you stand a far greater chance of seeing it published.

Schedule your work as before, if possible aim to deliver the completed manuscript to your publisher around the publication date of your first book. This is the time when you will be in your editor's thoughts and the work is more likely to have a favourable reading. Delivery of your new manuscript months afterwards could put it at a disadvantage; if your initial sales have been slow then your publishers might be hesitant to give you a favourable decision.

Who knows, a couple of good reviews on publication of Book One could result in a quick sale for Book Two!

You will not be in a position to push for an increased advance at this stage. You are still an unproven beginner. But don't accept a lower advance, that would be nothing less than exploitation by your publishers. Be content with a matching sum, and if the second book doesn't work out then at least you've doubled your money on your first!

Beware of 'rip-offs'

Shortly after the unexpected success of my *Night of the Crabs*, my publishers wrote to me and offered to commission another horror novel (unrelated to the Crabs, title and basic idea thought up editorially) for less money and a drop in royalty rates. I replied to the effect that I would be pleased to write the book if the terms equalled those of my previous one. A rather terse reply, by return of post, informed me that they were commissioning another author to write the book!

I learned here a basic lesson of the 1970s 'nasties' boom. A forthcoming major lead-title by a rival publisher needed to be countered by a similar book and I had been singled out to write it. 'Rip-offs' were all part of the game in those days and my future reputation could have been ruined by writing that book. It was a lucky let-off for me. Then, about three months later, my publishers offered me a new 2-book deal - on receipt of my ideas! Fortunately, nowadays publishers are far more discriminating in what they buy. Which is one reason why selling a book is so difficult.

Avoid déjà vu

Do try to add some variety to those horrific passages in your new book. Ensure that the victims meet with different fates, don't have them all killed in the same way - unless, of course, you are writing about a serial killer who operates to a pattern.

Make your second book different wherever you can; a fresh setting, introduce a few new and interesting characters. The last thing you want to create is déjà vu. Also, have a surprise ending, one that will fool those devotees of your previous book. Good does not always have to triumph over Evil, horror is no longer stereotyped. Even an on-going psychic detective has to lose occasionally. The plot must be credible even though you can get away with a lot in occult novels.

From now on each book you write should be better than your previous one. That comes from experience; the more you write, so should you improve, both in style and the art of story telling. Look back at the works of any of those prolific authors who have stood the test of time. In the very beginning they were no different from yourself, they encountered the same problems and anxieties. And they made it.

If you decide not to continue with a character or theme, then make your second book as different as possible from the first one. Otherwise you run the risk of being typecast into a particular niche. The horror field offers more variation and potential than almost any other.

Future success

It could be that your follow-up book is far more successful than your first. Any number of factors could influence that; a sharp decline in the publishing industry when your first book came out has now reversed and there is an upward spiral in sales, or perhaps a change of trend in the genre itself which you have fortunately followed. The latter can work for or against you, it's the luck of the draw.

Never attempt to forecast new trends, nor concentrate on something which is hitting the newspaper headlines at the time of writing. You could make a complete hash of the first and be a year too late with the second. Either way, you will not end up with a topical book, it will be out of fashion and will probably sink without trace.

Also bear in mind that if some real-life horror makes the news, a dozen or more horror writers like yourself will be trying to capitalize on it for their next book. Always search for that original idea.

Do not think a book ahead, you are not an established author yet. Devote all your efforts into the book you are currently writing, that way you will make a good job of it. Publishing is a slow business, the book you deliver now will not be published for 12-18 months. You will have ample time to concentrate on a third book when your editor has accepted your second.

May that elusive lucky break come your way!

Recommended reading

Many of these titles are no longer in print. It is worth checking libraries or secondhand bookshops for any that are unavailable in your local bookshop.

Arlen, Michael   *Hell! Said the Duchess*
Blackwood, Algernon   *The Empty House*
　John Silence
Bloch, Robert   *Psycho*
Boothby, Guy   *A Bid for Fortune*
Brandner, Gary   *The Howling*
Collins, Wilkie   *The Haunted Hotel*
De la Mare, Walter   *The Return*
Donovan, Dick   *The Scarlet Seal*
Doyle, Sir A. Conan   *The Horror of the Heights*
　　　　　　　　　　Lot 249
　　　　　　　　　　The Speckled Band
Fanthorpe, R. Lionel   *The Crawling Fiend* (as Bron Fane)
　　　　　　　　　　Softly by Moonlight (as Bron Fane)
　　　　　　　　　　The Attic (as Deutero Spartacus)
Hansby, J.J.   *The Creature From the Depths*
Hardy, R. & Shaffer, A   *The Wicker Man*
Horler, Sydney   *The Destroyer*
　　　　　　　The Curse of Doone
Jackson, Shirley   *The Haunting of Hill House*
King, Stephen   *The Shining*
Le Fanu, J. Sheridan   *Uncle Silas*
Lovecraft, H.P.   *Dagon*
　　　　　　　　The Shadow Over Innsmouth
Machen, Arthur   *The Bowmen*
Matheson, Richard   *I Am Legend*
　　　　　　　　　Shock
Poe, Edgar Allan   *The Premature Burial*
Rohmer, Sax   *Dr Fu Manchu* (all novels)
Shelley, Mary   *Frankenstein*
Stevenson, Robert Louis   *The Body Snatcher*
　　　　　　　　　　　The Strange Case of Dr Jekyll and Mr Hyde

Stoker, Bram   *Dracula*
Thomson, Christine Campbell (Ed)   *The 'Not at Night' Series*
(many *Weird Tales* reprints)
Wheatley, Dennis   *The Devil Rides Out*
The Satanist
To The Devil, A Daughter
Wellman, Manly Wade   *The Last Grave of Lil Warren*
Wollheim, Donald A. (Ed)   *Terror in the Modern Vein*
More Terror in the Modern Vein

I list here a selection of my own horror novels which illustrate the various trends of horror from 1974-96:

GOTHIC
Werewolf by Moonlight, 1974
Return of the Werewolf, 1977
The Son of the Werewolf, 1978

ANIMALS ON THE RAMPAGE
Night of the Crabs, 1976 (plus 5 sequels)
Bats Out of Hell, 1978
Locusts, 1979
Caracal, 1980

OCCULT
The Sabat series, 1982
The Neophyte, 1986
The Master, 1988

ECOLOGICAL DISASTERS
Abomination, 1986
The Plague Chronicles, 1993

PSYCHOLOGICAL
Phobia, 1990

HORROR/CRIME/SERIAL KILLERS
The Black Fedora, 1991
The Knighton Vampires, 1993
The Hangman, 1994 (as Gavin Newman)

'DARK' HORROR (Occult influence)
The Dark One, 1995
Dead End, 1995
The Cadaver, 1997

Useful addresses

British Fantasy Society
2 Harwood Street
Stockport SK4 1JJ

Contacts
(lists films, television production companies etc.)
7 Leicester Place
London WC2H 7BP
Tel: 0171-437 7631

Dark Horizons
(British Fantasy Soceity publication - publishes short fiction)
46 Oxford Road
Birmingham B28 6DT

The Dark Side
Stray Cat Publishing Limited
P.O. Box 146
Plymouth PL1 1AX

Forbidden Planet
(shop stocks wide selection of horror books and magazines)
71 New Oxford Street
London WC1A 1DG
Tel: 0171-836 4179

Graveyard Rendezvous
(official magazine of Guy N. Smith Fan club - publishes short horror stories, carries advice and features)
Sandra Sharp, Editor
Sheringham
West Street
Knighton
Powys LD7 1EN
Tel: (01547) 520551

Guy N. Smith Fan Club
Sandra Sharp, Organiser
Sheringham
West Street
Knighton
Powys LD7 1EN
Tel: (01547) 520551

Murder One
71–3 Charing Cross Road
London W2H 0AA
Tel: 0171–734 3483

Index